75 MUST-SEE
PLACES TO TAKE
THE KIDS
(BEFORE THEY DON'T WANT TO GO)

ROBIN ESROCK

Affirm
press

Dedicated to parents of young children everywhere,
because you all deserve a medal of accomplishment, a well-earned beer,
and a supportive hug. This book is the least I can do.
And, of course and as always, to Raquel and Galileo.

Published by Affirm Press in 2019
28 Thistlethwaite Street, South Melbourne, VIC 3205
www.affirmpress.com.au
10 9 8 7 6 5 4 3 2 1

A catalogue record for this
book is available from the
National Library of Australia

Title: 75 Must-See Places to Take the Kids (Before they don't want to go)
ISBN: 9781925712841 (paperback)

Cover design by Karen Wallis
Printed in China by C&C Offset Printing

All reasonable effort has been made to attribute copyright and credit.
Any new information supplied will be included in subsequent editions.

Disclaimer: Tourism is a constantly evolving industry. Hotels may change names,
restaurants may change owners and activities may no longer be available at all.
Records fall and facts shift. While a great deal of care has been taken to ensure that
the information provided is accurate as of the date the book was first sent to press,
the author and publisher disclaim responsibility for any harm or loss resulting from
reliance on information found in the book, or from the pursuit of any of the activities
described in the book.

Contents

Introduction

No parent of sound body and mind should consider, under any circumstances, travelling with young kids.

By young kids, I refer to individuals that require car seats and have not quite mastered the art of using the toilet (ranging in age from zero to thirty-five).

By travel, I'm not referring to camping trips, visiting relatives, or driving to the shopping centre. Rather, I specifically mean any act of lunacy that involves:

- Long flights in heavily confined spaces
- Sudden and disruptive toilet stops
- Sudden and disruptive projectile vomit
- Creative sleeping arrangements
- The ordeal of seeking out meals that match the cuisine of your child's imagination
- Long drives in heavily confined spaces
- Annoying, erratic and frustrating behaviour with no apparent cause
- Public transport
- Queues for expensive tourist attractions (some of which involve heavily confined spaces)
- Constant movement
- Bites – both insect-related (probably) and sibling-related (likely)

No. Don't even think of it. I mean, sure, it can be tempting, this idea of discovering exotic destinations together, bonding as a family, building memories to last several lifetimes.

But, like your decision to have offspring in the first place, so many things can go wrong. Risks include:

- Injury and death
- Illness and disaster
- Injury and death as a result of illness and disaster
- Scams and rip-offs

- Plane crashes and buses plunging into ravines
- Scams and rip-offs leading to plane crashes and buses plunging into ravines
- Losing your baggage
- Losing your children
- Losing yourself
- Losing your marriage (a different sort of baggage)
- Children being kidnapped
- Wives and husbands being kidnapped
- Wives and husbands kidnapping the children to go back home

Does it make sense to travel with young children? Not one iota. Will you do it, and have a blast anyway? Absolutely.

You get the idea.

It's a wonder that any parents would ever make the decision to travel with children in the first place. Hell, it's a wonder that parents would make the decision to *have* children in the first place. *What* a gamble! *What* a risk!

Therefore, it makes perfect sense to STAY AT HOME and NEVER GO ANYWHERE. Also, DON'T HAVE CHILDREN. Much safer, don't you think?

No?

No.

The truth is, having children makes no sense, and yet people like us do it anyway. It's kind of like skydiving. Does it make sense to jump out of a plane at 14,000 feet? Not one iota. Do people do it? Absolutely.

This is a book to inspire parents and would-be parents to travel, no matter how old their kids are. Does it make sense to travel with young children? Not one iota. Will you do it, and have a blast anyway? Absolutely.

A note for parents with older kids

By older kids I mean offspring with road awareness and the ability to dress themselves without intense negotiation, but without the capacity to earn their own money, figure out their own holidays and do important stuff, like vote and drink wine.

To beaten and bruised parents who've made it through toilet training, sleepless nights and tantrums, I trust you're enjoying the screen time warfare and sulking silences, punctuated by whining, complaining and eye-rolling. I see you, and I salute you. You are incredible. Well done, I can't wait to join you.

While sections of this book are aimed squarely at parents of five-and-unders (hence the references to car seats, naps and prams) you will still find the sections on screen time (p 296), where to stay (p 74), where to eat (p 220), how to travel on a budget (p 270) and how to keep kids interested on long drives (p 186) useful (particularly if you have kids at a range of ages).

On the other hand, you may have your travel routine down to a fine art, and just need some ideas for where to take your self-propelling offspring before they decide absolutely that they no longer wish to be anywhere near you. In which case proceed directly to your state of choice, pass GO and collect $200. Each experience has a universal appeal to delight different ages, interests, shapes and sizes. Maybe not thirteen-year-old girls though, as they belong in a category of their own.

I now invite you to step into this text box, and let me tell you a story.

I once found myself in northern Italy driving a Lamborghini, as one does. I was filming an episode for a TV show that took me to thirty-six countries to tick off my bucket list. It felt like a jolly amazing opportunity to visit both the Lamborghini and Ferrari factories, in Bologna and Modena respectively.

Keep in mind, as a young boy, I had a poster of a jet-blue Lamborghini Countach on my bedroom wall: driving a supercar was pretty high on the list of things I'd always wanted to do.

Under the guidance of a veteran test driver, I gripped the wheel of a Lamborghini Gallardo Spyder and expected angels with harps to light up the sky. Instead, I was beset by a feeling of . . . emptiness. You dream big and work hard to make your dreams come true, and then you realise that unless there's something a lot more meaningful than your own shallow drive for peak experiences (or fame and fortune), you will always feel the same disappointment.

It just so happened that my director for that episode had a six-month-old son, his first child. Peter couldn't stop gushing about his kid, how his son had changed everything for him, challenged him, inspired him, swept him up in indescribable joy.

After test-driving a Ferrari 430 Scuderia (sorry, the Lambo was better), I digested the day's experience over pizza and fine wine, and came to the following, somewhat naive conclusion: screw supercars. I want what Peter's got.

Three years later, my daughter was born, and three years after that, my son. I would continue to trade the ride in any supercar, along with all the adventures in the world, to experience the utter joy of *them*.

Although admittedly, the trade-off would hurt. A lot. Pizza, wine and super cars . . . in northern Italy? Oh well.

Having kids opens up a world of expensive, impractical and frustrating new realities. It also opens up a world of meaning, joy, deep appreciation, love and priceless inspiration.

It's easy to describe the challenges of parenting, but more existentially challenging to describe the rewards. All parents who don't eat their young will appreciate this. Suffice to say that, having ticked off just about every experience you can imagine all over the world, Peter the director was right: children make life worth living.

Like having kids, travel is expensive, impractical and full of risks. It is also one of the few things you can spend money on, as the famous saying goes, and become richer for your investment.

We travel because it is fun and meaningful. We travel because it teaches us about the world we live in, the people we share that world with and how to appreciate what – and who – we have. We travel because we must, and because our photos annoy the hell out of our friends on Facebook.

In these pages my young family will tackle every state and territory in

Australia at a feverish pace, learning about the remarkable experiences that put Down Under at the top of the world's great tourist destinations. There's much to share along the way, including amazing things to do and see, parenting tips (aka 'we made these terrible mistakes so you don't have to') and stories to inspire your own (mis)adventures.

Older parents often tell me the same thing: "Enjoy it while it lasts, because it goes by so quickly!" Before you know it – and before you've taken them to half the places you wanted to – your kids have grown up and gone. No more bedtime stories, no more morning cuddles, and no more of those special moments when you witness your kids evolve in real time. I've written several bucket list books to remind everyone that life passes us by faster than we realise. The opportunity to experience somewhere special with your adoring, wide-eyed kids goes by even faster. As older readers will confirm, parenting days might often feel long, but the years whiz past. Do it while you can, and, as the title of this book attests, do it while your kids want to do it too.

There is a real shortage of honest books about being a parent, and there are even fewer books about travelling with young kids. Oh, there's plenty of stuff out there about Perfect Parenting and raising Perfect Children. There are books with holier-than-thou advice from super parents who pack their kids in backpacks and trek to Kathmandu. Nobody talks about the time your kid took a dump in the bathtub with you, which was, in retrospect, a better experience than that time they took a dump in the hotel infinity pool.

It's okay. We survived, and so will you. As we travelled to every Australian state and territory, we found plenty of inspirational family travel moments, and you will too.

Robin Esrock

PS: Some readers might find this book to be a useful form of contraception.
   In which case, I apologise, and . . . you're welcome.

5

A short note on privacy

'I don't share any pictures of my children where you can clearly see their faces. After all, it will stay with them forever. And I never use their real names when I write about them publicly; after all, I have to respect their privacy.'
– Faceless parent blogger

Look, I get it. My entire third year of life is captured in just seven photographs, and here I have thirty-four photos of my kids just from this morning, plus GoPro footage, and all we did was visit a wildlife park to see Tasmanian devils grunt like nasally congested orcs at a Laotian ritual pig slaughter.

The internet never forgets. And yet, if a possibly inebriated Justin Trudeau can demonstrate in a YouTube clip how he can fall down a flight of stairs safely and still become the dashing Prime Minister of Canada, I believe my Canadian kids will be able to move forward in life without being haunted by the book their dad wrote when they were five and two years old.

Fact is, I simply cannot write a real book about real events without using real people. That said, I do apologise to my kids' future selves if the following stories cause them any embarrassment. It's not their fault that their father is a travel writer, but hey, there are definite perks!

Nevertheless, I have chosen to respect my children's privacy by referring to my daughter as 'Raquel' and my son as 'Galileo' in this book. It is merely a coincidence that their actual names are Raquel and Galileo.

Since these names will come up repeatedly, an introduction is appropriate.

The family

Raquel turned five years old midway through our year-long travel adventure. Strangers constantly stop her to compliment or tussle her hair, which is wild, corkscrewed and curly.

In Thailand, people felt compelled to reach out and touch it, which is odd because touching a stranger's head in Thailand is a strict no-no. You can lose yourself – along with small toys and occasionally scrambled egg – in Raquel's hair.

Are kids with straight hair more straight-laced, or are they also capable of charming the fur off a koala one moment, and nuking the poor marsupial with an epic meltdown the next? Euphemistically, parents of children like Raquel refer to them as 'spirited'. She is strong-willed and bull-headed, and a classic temperamental Aries.

She is also too smart, too aware and uncannily expressive. She can emotionally break a babysitter before tea, and cuddle up like a sweetheart at bedtime. Raquel does not eat much, does not sleep much and literally shakes with excitement, frustration, anger and joy, sometimes all at the same time.

If you don't have one of these kids, consider yourself spared. For those who do, God help us.

Yes, we named our son Galileo. I'd tell you the long genesis of his impressive name, but it isn't really that interesting. Neither my wife nor myself are scientifically inclined and, as creative types, we're hoping Gali's name will set him on an accomplished path like rocket science, as opposed to, say, playing drums in a shitty garage band.

Travelling for a year from eighteen months old and onward, Gali started off measured and calm. He is expressive and curious, but likes his privacy, frequently closing doors so he can play alone in a dark room, or a car trailer.

He eats well and sleeps well, at least, when he's not growth spurting or behaving like a little tyrant, which all two year olds are wont to do.

'If I could guarantee we'd have another Gali, I'd have more kids,' my wife says. He's one of *those* kids, which is just as well, because two Raquels would surely have done us in.

Of course, Gali's behaviour did change dramatically towards the end of our trip, when he realised he was two years old, which gave him licence to headbutt our groins,

punch our throats, throw himself to the floor in dramatic tantrums, toss his food, lick aeroplane carpets and generally behave like a two year old. His sister clearly served as an outstanding role model.

Ana, or Mom to the little ones, is from Rio de Janeiro, and her blood runs tropically hot. Ana will be the first to tell you that she's no natural-born Earth mother, happy to change a poopy nappy with one hand while whipping up freshly squeezed organic blood orange juice with the other.

Motherhood has come naturally to her the same way fatherhood has come naturally to me: with unnerving and exhausting challenges. Like so many other mums and dads, life dumped us both in the parenting deep end and we're figuring out how not to drown, even if it means we have to occasionally stand on each other's heads to get some air.

Before kids, Ana used to work in a brewery, and carnival danced in high heels with feathers on her head. These days, she drinks a lot of coffee, wears flats and exclaims how much easier it would be if kids were as light as feathers.

Ana is always prepared with exactly the kind of parenting solution we needed *last* time, but she never stops trying. Chronically sleep-deprived, she is just now beginning to realise all the amazing things we got up to with the kids in Australia . . . and we arrived home three months ago.

This book, along with our children, would not have happened without her. That's a statement of acknowledgment, by the way, not blame.

As for me, I have travelled to more than one hundred countries on seven continents chasing the extraordinary, all the while writing, photographing and broadcasting

9

my discoveries in print, television and online. This prepared me for parenthood the way making fruit salad prepares you for advanced veterinary surgery.

I have never had a single serious incident in all my journeys: no weird illness, no robberies or theft, no attacks or muggings. I credit this fact to trusting my instinct, breathing, smiling, trying not to take things too seriously and remaining calm.

Unfortunately, that doesn't seem to work with the kids, who have infected me with their mystery playground germs, stolen my disposable income and left me defenceless against constant attacks of cuteness and curiosity.

I agreed to write this book at the same time as writing a grown-up version titled *The Great Australian Bucket List*.

I accepted the assignment of writing two books on an insane schedule because I love challenges, travel adventures and apologising to car sponsors for mysterious, carrot-like substances permanently fused with expensive leather interiors.

Disclaimer

Every book about parenting does the same thing. There you are, looking for trustworthy answers, something to explain the spots, a reason your kid has developed a taste for radish stems or easy suggestions on how to apply sunscreen to eyeballs.

What does that book/website always say? Every child is *different*. Just because it works for this kid, doesn't mean it will work for that kid. Oh, and the spots are either the pox or pimples, your kid is eating radish stems because he/she is lacking iron, apply eyeball sunscreen through the rectal cavity – and oh, it's highly possible your child has an incredibly rare form of cancer, or is absolutely normal.

Since nobody knows much about anything, the publisher and author therefore take no responsibility for any and all advice, or what might happen if you pursue the activities in this book. Because if there's one thing we can reliably count on, it's that every child, along with every adventure, will be different.

FEAR OF FLYING WITH KIDS

There's a very simple secret to flying, a hushed truth that travel experts rarely reveal: if you want to remove the stress, go to the airport *early*.

The check-in counters are quiet, there are no sweaty dashes for the gate, you can enjoy a fine beverage, look at social media or read a book guilt free – because what the hell else are you supposed to do for ninety minutes in an airport?

You might even do some shopping, but remember, there's nothing free about duty free. Then board your flight, and unless you're being productive and catching up on some work, you can happily binge watch a TV series, load up on a few plane movies, read, sleep or drink, or do of all these at the same time.

I like flying. Cruising 38,000 feet in the air at 900 kilometres an hour is quite a remarkable thing to do, especially when you consider your relative comfort, access to beverages and proximity away from the folks seated in rows thirty-four to thirty-eight. Those poor, *poor* bastards.

Today, fate has decided to put a family with two kids under five in row thirty-six . . . on a sixteen-hour flight. Those kids are not going to sleep blissfully or lose themselves binge watching Pixar movies.

No, those kids are going to whine, scream and vibrate with the injustice of having to endure sixteen hours in a tiny little seat, and there's absolutely nothing anyone can do about it. I know this, because those kids are mine.

• • • • • • • • • • • • • • • • • • •

THE LONG HAUL

As you're fully aware, Australia is quite isolated, especially if you're flying to Europe or North America, or swimming in from Asia. Our big Aussie family adventure commenced with a sixteen-hour nightmare, also known as the direct flight from Vancouver to Melbourne.

We took all the precautions: packed snacks, games, toys, apps on the iPad, videos, colouring books . . . all of which took care of the *first* hour. Sixteen hours on a plane once meant I could watch romantic comedies (the ones you *only* watch on planes when nobody can see you tear up).

With young kids, however, each minute is a volcano threatening to erupt in tears and overtired tantrums. So we walked the kids to the front of the plane, we walked the kids to the back of the plane. We endured episodes of crying and thrashing about, and the hairy judging eyeballs of neighbouring passengers, especially those with no kid experience.

The Children Divide becomes obvious and enormous on long-haul flights. Parents of young kids will acknowledge each other with sighs of solidarity, like soldiers marching to the battlefield knowing we're about to be mowed down by machine guns loaded with breast milk.

Parents of older kids are sympathetic and annoyingly smug with eyes that express: 'I've been there, it sucks, *but* it's not me this time, so I'm going to order another vodka and tonic and queue up the romantic comedy'. Older people or travelling professionals are just cranky, but they're that way regardless.

It's the childless who feel the most hard done by, barely able to restrain their indignation, aiming their judgement like marbles in a catapult. Their eyes yell: 'If that was my kid, I'd have them under control!' and 'You're a crap parent!' and 'Who do you think you are, bringing children on *my* plane?!'

Every parent knows what it feels like to be at the receiving end of this, but it is easily resolved. Great relief will come if you follow this single, simple step: brush it off and screw the lot of them.

There, doesn't that feel great? Say it again, and this time you could make it a duet with your partner. '*Screw*. Them!'

Airborne parenting judges cannot possibly understand what you have been through, are going through and will go through. They do not appreciate that getting out the front door was a major accomplishment in itself. Judgemental passengers cannot appreciate how you'd gladly trade for the three farting passengers in front of them *plus* the seat by the toilet if it would mean you could have ten minutes without a kid clinging to your neck.

You're in that special kind of hell called a Long-haul Flight With Young Children, and the last thing you need is to feel like you're a shitty parent. This is why 'screw them!' will become your mantra.

Yes, screw them all. Except perhaps the sweet granny in row thirty-nine, who offered to hold your infant while you peed and your partner wrestled the demon toddler.

Don't worry, in fourteen hours and fifty-nine minutes it will all be over. And by over, I mean you still have to line up for customs, baggage claim, taxis and the hotel reception.

Long-haul flights are the price you might have to pay for giving your kids experiences that will fashion them into interesting and curious people. Although, every time we disembark from a long-haul flight, my wife proclaims that we will *never*, *ever* do this again.

But we will, because parents of young children are sleep-deprived, and as such, have no short-term memory. You won't take much comfort in the seat, meal or experience, but take comfort in this: once it's over, it's over.

THE SHORT HAUL

Take the long haul, subtract eleven to fifteen hours, and there you have it. If at all possible, avoid red-eye or early-morning flights, because it's never *just* a one-hour flight, it's the two hours on either end of that flight – not to mention any connections – that will bite you like a rabid red-back spider.

Arrive early to avoid the stress and let the kids explore the airport, the better examples of which have small playgrounds. Short-haul flights themselves can be soaked up with the toys, devices, snacks and overall thrill of the experience. At least the first ten minutes of them.

TIPS FOR FLYING

Screens

Some studies suggest that young children should not be exposed to screen time before the age of two. Others suggest that screen time must be limited and always monitored.

On a long-haul flight, do not even *think* about those studies. The tablet or smartphone is your friend. Load up your friend with shows you know your child will be glued to.

Take an old smartphone destined for the back of a drawer and turn it into your kid's toy, since it's not much good for anything else, and you won't be devastated when it is inevitably broken or lost.

A family of five we met told us they lost a new iPad on the first flight of a five-month trip. We forgot our old iPhone 3 in the pouch of our first long-haul flight from Canada. The good news is you only make that expensive mistake once.

Before the flight, do your best to keep the screen for the plane and not while waiting for the plane. Much like anaesthesia, you want its full impact when you need it most.

The older kids get, the more they'll park their eyes in front of a screen. Yes, it's probably not good for their neural circuits, mental development or eyeballs, but when it comes to travelling with kids, this is called progress.

Snacks

When you notice your kid chewing on a tray table that was last wiped down in 1989, pull out a snack. Dried fruit, crackers, popcorn, baked pea thingies – anything that won't stick to your sock when you step on it, because most of this snack will inevitably end up on the floor.

Make sure the snacks are easily accessible and you don't have to dig too far into the kid's bag to find it, and pack them in Ziploc bags. We hate single-use plastic, but these are special circumstances; you can save the Earth later.

Bags

It's a good idea to bring at least one bag on board with just the kids' stuff. Books, snacks, stuffed animals, toys.

It's important, however, *not* to bring too much stuff, which will eat up your baggage allowance. If you're travelling with more than one kid, give them each a colourful bag. Doing so will allow them to keep all their stuff together, feel a sense of ownership, have their own baggage allowance and exhibit a sense of entitlement when they inevitably ask you to carry it.

Toys

Avoid toys with lots of pieces, unless you want to crawl all over a sticky carpet picking them up. Avoid playdough, because it will get everywhere, and airline cleaning staff will put a hex on you.

Kids have the attention spans of squirrels on methamphetamines, so variety is key. We had great success with a box of little plastic animals, with each new horse or cow promising a new adventure in the twelve seconds before it fell to the floor or got stuck between seats.

Colouring-in books, flash cards and stickers are useful and cheap to replenish. When it comes to toys, less can be more, which is why you're better off downloading educational apps and movies, and letting the screen do all the work.

Medication

Some parents speak highly of travel medications. Ethically, each can draw their own line as to whether drugging is worth the peace that follows. Peace or disaster, as some drugs can have the opposite effect to the one intended, causing far more grief than they are worth. I'm talking about drugs for us parents, of course. We would never drug our kids . . . too often.

Boarding

You may be tempted to get on the plane as soon as possible to get your nightmare underway. Civilised airlines give priority boarding to parents travelling with young families.

A good tip is to board and deplane in the least stressful manner for your kids. Ideally, this would mean not at all, but since that is not an option, take your time. A popular parenting travel trip is to let everyone board first so you spend the least amount of time possible on the plane.

This is ideal for empty red-eye flights, but only prolongs the suffering on busy flights, and denies you valuable space in the overhead bins.

Toilets and hygiene

You will have all the proof you'll ever need about the robust resilience of the human body after a long-haul flight with a small child.

Given the tray licking, floor rolling and toilet-seat dive, you'd expect your kids to emerge at your destination beset by a flesh-eating disease. Somehow, this is not the case. Still, pack hand sanitiser and plenty of wipes if it will make you feel better about yourself.

Check-ins

Depending on security and staff, we often skipped long lines at check-in or customs, using our kids as an excuse. Many airports recognise the benefits of getting screaming, overtired kids processed first and have a separate line for families, although this is not always clearly marked.

For some reason, arrivals and check-in halls are designed to echo and increase the decibels of a toddler's high-pitched wail, which is something to always use to your advantage when jostling to check in.

Clothing

Both parents and children should fly with comfortable layers and slip-ons, and avoid buttons, glitter prints, zippers, laces, hard screen prints, safety pins or anything that will cause discomfort as you twist yourself into a pretzel to keep blood flowing to vital body parts.

If you expect the plane to be warm, it will be colder than the Snowy Mountains in winter, and if you expect it to be cold, it will be hotter than a steam sauna in Darwin.

Prepare for both eventualities,

using any thin blankets provided to pad armrests or catch vomit – sometimes at the same time. I highly recommend compression socks for long-haul flights, which work wonders for circulation.

Seating

Kids and aisle seats are not a good combination. Not only are kids at risk of losing a limb from beverage and food carts, but it also gives them ample opportunity to escape to the cockpit and cause an international security incident. Should your kids finally fall asleep, carefully thread the seatbelt around them to avoid flight attendants asking you to wake them up when the seatbelt sign comes on mid-flight for no fathomable reason.

I appreciate flight attendants have a job, but waking kids up when they finally and *at last* fall asleep puts everyone's mental health at risk.

Remain calm

Exhaustion, frustration and lack of sleep all threaten to make a bad situation worse, with terrible decision-making and regretful consequences.

No matter how much a passenger annoys you, do not lash out physically or you may well find yourself restrained and in trouble with the authorities. I'm talking to both parents and children here.

The koala *Phascola...* ...s a marsupial mammal
found only here in ...

Koalas are totally d... ...llands ; they live in
trees and feed mai...

Follow the par...
about this fas...

VICTORIA

EUREKA SKYDECK

Down with acrophobia

 Age minimum: None

 Open: Year round

 Visit: www.eurekaskydeck.com.au

It's fun to get high, and given what parents go through, who can blame us? Observation decks are the best places to go if you're after a rush, and you can bring the kids along too.

Located in Southbank, Melbourne's Eureka Tower is the second-tallest building in the country, and was briefly the tallest residential building in the world. At eighty-eight floors high, the Eureka Skydeck is the highest observation deck in the southern hemisphere, and while we're bestowing accolades, the elevator to get there is the fastest in the hemisphere, too.

The 360-degree view around Melbourne is impressive, and your kids can happily and safely run circles around the deck to burn off the ice-cream you'll inevitably buy them from the kiosk. There's an outside viewing area as well, which is frequently windy and conveniently fenced in, although that won't stop your knees from shaking in the breeze!

Children are not born with a fear of heights. Research has shown that infants develop a healthy fear of heights from life experience, not from innate survival hardwiring. As infants grow, they learn more about their bodies and become more perceptive, and tend to stop doing stupid things like walking off cliffs.

Point is, neuropsychologists believe that an acute fear of heights only develops with a combination of a bad experience and gradual learned behaviour. This fact is

important to bear in mind as you lead your kids into the glass box that extends three metres out the side of the Eureka Tower, 300 metres in the air.

This protruding glass cavity is called The Edge, and if you freak out inside it, you might just instil a lifelong fear of heights in your little ones. Keep your cool, on the other hand, and you might well encourage a future skydiver or bungee jumper to take a leap of faith! Either way, this is one of the few definite thrills that parents and young kids can enjoy together, so it's worth the scary step inside.

When you first step into the cube, it is opaque. A mechanism slowly extends it from the building, and then a speaker blasts a cracking glass sound effect as the opaque windows magically clear to reveal the city beneath your feet. Never mind the heights, this dramatic reveal could just as well give your kids a lifelong fear of sound effects! My kids looked at the glass floor, walls and ceiling and didn't seem the least bit bothered. Then again, they are *my* kids.

We took some photos and after a minute or two, my five year old got a little antsy. A couple of months later she conquered a high-ropes course and wanted to scramble up the world's highest tree climb.

So I give thanks to the Eureka Skydeck. Not only does it offer memorable views of Melbourne, a speedy elevator and an excuse to visit the waterfront promenade of Southbank, but it also quite possibly dispels the irrational fear of heights that might plague your kids for the rest of their lives.

MELBOURNE ZOO
ROAR 'N' SNORE

Wild in the dark

 Age minimum: Five years. Kids under eighteen years must be accompanied by an adult

 Open: Weekend evenings September to May

 Visit: www.zoo.org.au/melbourne/wild-encounters/roar-n-snore

In summer, Melbourne Zoo gets about 10,000 visitors a day. All of them had gone home when my daughter and I pulled into the car park at 6pm. The gates were shut, and knowing the assortment of wild animals that resided behind them, it felt like we were starring in a Hollywood movie, the kind where lions escape their cages and start picking off overnight tourists one by one.

To be fair, young kids will likely be less concerned with the animals and more freaked out by the dark, since they rarely spend much time in it – never mind roaming around a deserted zoo to a soundtrack of grunts, hisses and growls in near blackness.

The service gates opened, and the group of just over a dozen Roar 'n' Snorers met our two friendly hosts for the evening : Jacky and Katheryn were fun, enthusiastic, knowledgeable, and superb role models for my five year old. We drove our vehicles into the service area backstage at the zoo and were shown to safari-style canvas tents on raised wooden platforms.

Shaded by palm trees and within earshot of various animal calls, our tents were surprisingly

roomy, with sleeping bags, pillows and air mattresses provided. We were advised to keep the tents zipped unless we wanted to cuddle a possum, which, I had to remind my daughter, is *not* something we *actually* wanted to do.

Having dropped off our bags, we were led on a behind-the-scenes tour of the zoo, learning about the animals' diets and the old heritage-listed buildings that now function as storage facilities. The older kids in the group were captivated, but mine just wanted to see animals. Fortunately, the red panda was up and about, and eager to say

hello on our short walk to the public bathrooms. With fruit bats flying overhead, we were free to wander about while our hosts prepared grilled burgers and chicken, served with salads and corn in a former elephant enclosure.

Satiated, we grabbed our headlamps and headed out for a nocturnal walk in the zoo; animals are always more lively at night. We hurled apples and pears to the elephants, greeted the hyperactive Bolivian squirrel monkeys, and learned it was best to keep our distance from the dangerous and unpredictable one-eyed tapir.

27

Parents with kids who run on a tight schedule might struggle with the late bedtime, but older kids will have a much easier go of it. After breakfast, we took a pre-opening excursion to handfeed the giraffe, and watched a zookeeper feed the penguins. Roar 'n' Snore tickets include admission for the following day so you can retrace your steps in the early-morning sun before the zoo opens for business. There are similar zoo sleepover programs in several zoos around the country, all making for a memorable and wild night out in the urban jungle.

Along the way, our hosts told us interesting stories about the animals, and revealed the fascinating inner workings of the zoo. At the lion enclosure, a juvenile male big cat was particularly active and jumped up against the thick glass viewing area. I don't think he was looking for cuddles.

As the smallest and therefore most vulnerable member of our group, my daughter clung to my neck for the remainder of the walk. It was dark, late, a little spooky, and it was time to go to bed. Milk and cookies were the reward back at our camp.

The Best Zoos in Australia

Most zoos offer an overnight or behind-the-scenes tour, allowing kids to encounter wildlife's greatest hits across the country.

1. Melbourne Zoo, Victoria

2. Taronga Zoo Sydney, New South Wales

3. Australia Zoo, Queensland

4. Adelaide Zoo, South Australia

5. Monarto Zoo, South Australia

6. Taronga Western Plains Zoo, New South Wales

7. Currumbin Wildlife Sanctuary, Queensland

tarantulas for the entire day. The museum is free for kids under sixteen and reasonably priced for adults – a no-brainer for travelling families. Across town in the industrial area of Spotswood is Scienceworks. Also administered by Museums Victoria, Scienceworks is more than just an interactive educational facility: it's the kind of place that makes you *feel* like a great parent, taking the time to teach your kids great things.

They'll have a blast learning about electricity, biology and space travel, and so will you. The Ground Up exhibition is targeted squarely at babies to five year olds, and my kids would have been content to stay and play there all afternoon. Like lizards basking in sunshine, I doubt they would have moved from the switchboard contraption and air tubes.

Sportsworks challenges kids to run and jump and throw, jump on a snowboard or in a canoe, and tests their reflexes and flexibility. Older kids will have a field day with all of this, while younger kids will likely view the experience as a particularly fun playground where they get to do lots of very out-of-the-ordinary stuff.

It costs a little extra for the onsite Planetarium and Lightning Room (perhaps a little too 'shocking' for the young ones), and there's an onsite café for lunch if you want to make a day of it. Call ahead and ask if there are school trips planned that day, as it can get busy. If so, plan a visit in the afternoon when the buses leave and your kids won't have to line up in frustration. Both museums are ideal for rainy days or unpredictable weather, which is just about any day in Melbourne!

NATIONAL GALLERY OF VICTORIA (NGV)

But is it art?

 Age minimum: None

 Open: Year round, closed Christmas Day

 Visit: www.ngv.vic.gov.au

Divided across two striking buildings – NGV International on St Kilda Road and NGV Australia in Federation Square – Melbourne's premier art galleries are kid-friendly with plenty of space to burn hours and energy, providing your toddler doesn't rugby tackle the bronze Rodin statue (in which case, budget for many more hours and energy trying to pay it off).

As is the case with most art galleries, you're going to want to keep your kids under control and engaged with the impressive displays of creativity that surround them, but steady yourself for the fact they might not be the least bit impressed with Van Gogh or Picasso. Impressionist squiggly lines are not nearly as cool as dinosaurs or horses.

Andy Warhol's bright colours did seem to have an immediate impact on the toddlers, something I'm sure Andy would be proud of. The NGV offers regular children's programs to encourage creative drawing and expression, and to shift the entertainment responsibility so parents can enjoy some relief, at least for an hour.

Kids' activity sheets are available at the front desk, the hallways

and galleries are supremely pram-friendly, and there is a general calming, quiet ambiance. Worth noting are the Great Hall and NGV Garden for spaces where kids can go a little nuts without eliciting condemnatory glares from adults debating the dollar value of art in hushed tones.

The NGV scores big bonus points for the free entry, and kids under five attend ticketed shows for free as well. My kids loved the circular Star Trekkian NGV International elevator and the nineteenth-century European paintings gallery, which features a lot of horses along with an inexplicable number of nudes. Speaking of which, be grateful the NGV is not the Vancouver Art Gallery, which goes by the moniker of VAG. When visitors to Canada

overhear me tell my wife, Ana, that I'm going to slip into the VAG because I've got nothing better to do, you'd think they have no appreciation for art history whatsoever.

GAME DAY AT THE MCG

Be a good sport

 Age minimum: None

 Open: Year round, museum and tours closed Melbourne Cup Day, Good Friday and Christmas Day

 Visit: www.mcg.org.au

It wasn't my intention to take my five year old to the opening day of the Boxing Day Ashes at the MCG. I called everyone I knew to be my plus one, but they either couldn't make it or equated the idea of watching test cricket to watching snails wrestle.

Dads the world over experience the unique pleasure of indoctrinating their kids into the cult of their favourite sports – the joy and agony of the deciding matches and the distinct thrill of joining tens of thousands of other lunatics at a big event, more engaged in a largely meaningless game than we would ever be in, say, domestic politics. Speaking of politics, protest marches are a fun day out with the kids too (provided you're in Australia, and not, say, Tehran). There was no protest from Ana, though, when I offered to take our daughter Raquel to the opening day of the Ashes. Hell, my wife would have been thrilled if I had kept Raquel busy for the full five days of the match.

So we made our way to the Melbourne Cricket Ground, the country's most hallowed sporting arena, filtering through fans of the

Barmy Army and the far happier Australian supporters, since the Baggy Greens had already won the series. By the time we arrived, the match was underway, but the journey made my daughter hungry. A carton of overpriced chips and bottle of water in hand, we almost made it to our seats when Raquel told me she needed to pee. We located the nearest bathrooms to find a queue of sloshed punters had already formed before noon, and of course I couldn't take her into the ladies', which would have undoubtedly been more civilised.

Fortunately, there were wheelchair-access toilets, which have come to parents' rescue many a time. *Un*fortunately, there was a bunch of sloshed punters lining up for that one too. I politely told the three guys in front of me that if my daughter didn't go in next, she would piss all over them.

The desperate look on her face must have convinced them we meant business. We got into the stall to find a toilet seat so wet with urine you could float a rubber duck on it, but my daughter showed me a lady trick her mum had taught her

involving a well-positioned squat.

Finally, we returned to take our seats. Australia's opening batters were in and settled, and despite the 80,000 people cheering them on, there wasn't much action. A minute and a half later, my daughter interrupted my attempt to explain the rules of cricket by telling me she was bored and wanted to go outside.

She repeated this refrain every twelve seconds for the next ten minutes. We left our seats and went for a walk around the stadium, relieved that Cricket Australia had conveniently and thoughtfully set up batting tents, catching pillows and other activities to keep kids entertained. Meanwhile, their dads stood around wondering why the hell they decided to bring their kids to the game in the first place.

An hour later, we headed back into the stadium and located our seats, where we managed to catch the only fifteen minutes worth catching that day. The Aussie opening batter was caught on ninety-nine, sending the Barmy Army into a frenzy and the dejected batter back to the team pavilion.

Then the big screen showed the bowler had overstepped the line – a technical no ball. The batter returned and scored his century, running into the outfield and leaping for joy. It was a magical moment as the crowd relished another memorable opportunity to stick it to the Brits, which is really the point of the entire Ashes series anyway.

Shortly after play continued, my daughter was ready to go outside again, since the batting nets were far more fun. We never got back to our seats. Still, the MCG delivered its magic, and our visit to the onsite National Sports Museum was more successful. Don't miss any opportunity to bond with your kids through sport, in any stadium, whatever the outcome and however old they are. Even if your mates are busy.

SOVEREIGN HILL

Into the time machine

 Age minimum: None

 Open: Year round, closed Christmas Day

 Visit: www.sovereignhill.com.au

Toddlers and infants don't need self-help books to remind them to live in the moment. Masters of not so subtly not giving a f**k, their attitudes epitomise the *here* and *now*. Talk to them about the great Victorian gold rush, and it shares mental space with dinosaurs and the time they headbutted Mum in the groin.

All this makes a visit to Sovereign Hill, a sprawling open-air museum and one of Victoria's biggest tourist attractions, less about the history, and more about the stuff your kids can actually do. Fortunately, there's a lot to do, and most of it is included in your ticket price.

I set up our visit by telling my kids we were going through a time machine. On the other end of the ticketing and gift shop, I told them, was a wormhole that would transport us back to 1850, right into the heart of Ballarat's gold boom. A wormhole, I explained, is what you get when you eat too many gummy worms, which creates a magical gate to the days before Grandma's Grandma was born.

As we entered, the painstaking

detail of Sovereign Hill's replica nineteenth-century streets instantly captured the kids' imagination. Walking into the stores on Main Street, we interacted with costumed actors who took special delight chatting to the kids.

In the photography studio, we slipped on period costumes (you can never go wrong with dress-up!). If only we could have kept the clothes for the visit and gone full *Westworld*, albeit a *Westworld* devoid of psychopaths and sentient robots.

Over the course of the day, we watched the traditional production of a wooden wagon wheel, which sounds less interesting than it was, and saw blacksmith demonstrations and red coats parading in formation by the square. We popped into replica housing full of antique furniture, and played with chickens and goats.

A Clydesdale horseride around town delighted the kids, while holding a gold bar worth $160,000 delighted us adults. The kids soon found themselves in an old-fashioned candy store, learning about the art and production of

traditional lollies, and tasting a few too.

As we wandered about the sixty-plus historic buildings, I noticed that nobody wanted to look at a smart-phone, which would have shattered the illusion and fun of time travel. Promised the rewards of a gold flake (preserved in a bottle of water for a few dollars), the kids panned for gold in a little creek.

After a few hours at Sovereign Hill's manicured, life-sized tribute to the past, you'll no doubt wonder if life was truly better back then, before on-demand entertainment, pesticides and social media. Of course, this was also before antibiotics, pasteurised milkshakes and washer-dryers.

Still, Sovereign Hill is a fun living history lesson that will infuse your kids with curiosity and wonder about their history. For, despite their affinity for the present, learning from the past will ultimately help them navigate a successful future.

ARTPLAY

Swinging around the CBD

 Age minimum: None

 Open: Playground year round, activities Wednesday to Sunday

 Visit: www.melbourne.vic.gov.au/arts-and-culture/artplay/Pages/artplay.aspx

There's a lot of action in Melbourne's CBD. Buskers and street vendors, crowds swelling in and out of the malls and arcades, trams, tourists, cafes, storefronts and restaurants. Adults might be content to wander about taking it all in, but kids will need to blow off some steam, preferably in a location where they won't be trampled by crowds or public transport.

Located behind Federation Square on the north bank of the Yarra, ArtPlay is an inspired city investment designed for kids and artists to express ideas and let their creativity run amok. Targeting kids twelve and under, it includes the only playground in the city with slides, sandpits, swinging hammocks, climbing features and balance beams.

Open Wednesday to Sunday, an onsite creative arts studio led by local artists runs workshop programs that include ceramics, mosaics, puppetry, circus, collage, singing, sculpture and dance. Booking ahead for these programs is essential, although there are free drop-in workshops as well.

Anchored by a restored red-brick industrial building, the space is large and well lit with large windows overhead, hosting some 300 events each year in partnership with various community organisations and art groups.

The playground itself is a free-for-all and free-to-all, which gets particularly busy with school groups during the week. There are shade sails and an onsite coffee shop (this is Melbourne after all) where you can get off your feet while your kids get busy on theirs, exploring the steep walkways, wobbly rope bridge and sandpit.

For more terrific playgrounds in Melbourne, visit Royal Park Nature Playground (voted the best playground in the country by the Australian Institute of Landscape Architects), Queens Park in Moonee Ponds and the lovely Royal

Botanic Gardens on the Yarra's south bank.

Alternatively, you could take your kids on a tour of Melbourne's most famous coffee shops, but you'll probably be asked to leave when they start swinging around the neck of the barista.

Top 10 Playgrounds in Australia

1. Riverside Green, South Bank, Brisbane, Queensland

2. Glenelg Foreshore Playspace, Glenelg, South Australia

3. Denham Foreshore Playground, Shark Bay, Western Australia

4. Bellerive Beach Park, Hobart, Tasmania

5. Yokine Playground, Yokine, Western Australia

6. Pod Playground, National Arboretum, Canberra, Australian Capital Territory

7. Darling Quarter, Sydney, New South Wales

8. Rio Tinto Naturescape Kings Park, Perth, Western Australia

9. Wulaba Park, Waterloo, Sydney, New South Wales

10. Lizard Log Nature Playground, Western Sydney, New South Wales

BRIGHTON
BATHING BOXES

Colour on the sand

 Age minimum: None

 Open: Year round

 Visit: www.brightonbathingbox.org.au

Dendy Street Beach in Brighton, about a half-hour from the Melbourne CBD, remains one of the most popular seaside attractions in the city. The sand is soft, the bay-sheltered water is calm and the beach is framed by one of the city's more eccentric attractions: eighty-two colourfully painted bathing boxes lined up in a row, facing west to toast every sunset.

Their timber frames and corrugated-iron roofs are a reminder of Victorian sensibilities, when 'morality boxes' were built to protect modesty, house people's knick-knacks and provide shade, comfort and privacy during beach excursions.

Today, these privately owned boxes are uniquely painted, providing a lovely backdrop to a modern beach excursion (where bare skin no longer causes the stir it once did). Unfortunately, they are not available to rent, and if you want to own one, prepare to shell out upwards of $300,000 for a wooden box the size of a backyard shed. At 2.4 metres by 2 metres by 2 metres, this is some of the priciest real estate in Melbourne!

Rarely available and handed down across generations, it's quite the status symbol to own a box, as we discovered when we were graciously allowed to use one. As the kids played in the shallow seawater lapping metres from our little patio, tourists from around the world stopped to chat and ask us questions.

Eating our supermarket-procured picnic in the precious shade of Box 43, sandwiched between popular rainbow-painted boxes that drew the attention of everyone with an Instagram account, we felt like beach royalty. Unless you've got some sweet local contacts, you'll have to content yourself with the beach and the famous backdrop, both of which are well worth the visit.

ASHCOMBE MAZE & LAVENDER GARDENS

Roam to a gnome

 Age minimum: None, although the maze and some of the trails are not pram-friendly

 Open: Year round

 Visit: www.ashcombemaze.com.au

It's the oldest and best-known hedge maze in Australia, located within twenty-five acres of gardens where conifers and deciduous trees tower three metres high and up to two metres thick. Ashcombe was the first of several mazes we visited across the country, and we made the mistake of thinking it would be child's play.

Oh, adults can definitely get lost in these hedges, which is fun times, until your kid tells you she needs to use the toilet, like, *now*. A number one or number two? She's not sure either, sorry!

With its forty-year-old hedges, Ashcombe is a gorgeous-looking maze: lush, dreamy and curvy. Manicuring nature is a constant chore, and depending on your visit, some of the gardens might be in full bloom, and others not so much.

As with all family travel, it's best to lower your expectations of a top-notch adult attraction and just let the kids enjoy being outside and exploring a different space. Our kids loved the Great Gnome Hunt and Woodland Fairy Walk, tracking down the nine garden gnomes and nine fairies scattered throughout the gardens and lavender fields. One fairy had a 'conversation' with our five year old for five blessed minutes. Raquel told us she was the only one who could hear the little winged creature, and who are we to argue?

Surrounded by the fragrance

49

of lavender approaching bloom, the kids spent a good deal of time banging on the wind chimes and running about the ten uniquely themed gardens, before we headed to the Ashcombe Maze Café for a fresh-baked veggie quiche and some homemade lavender ice-cream.

Ashcombe may not be the biggest or most impressive maze in the country, and the gardens are a little rough about the edges, but it's a lovely opportunity to while away a few hours, letting the kids get lost in conversation with flowers and fairies

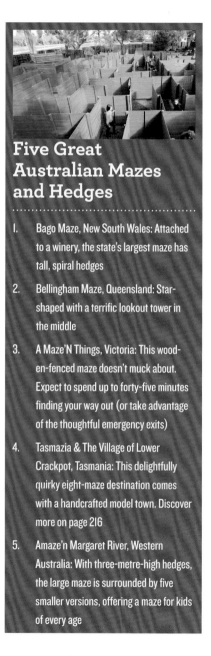

Five Great Australian Mazes and Hedges

1. Bago Maze, New South Wales: Attached to a winery, the state's largest maze has tall, spiral hedges

2. Bellingham Maze, Queensland: Star-shaped with a terrific lookout tower in the middle

3. A Maze'N Things, Victoria: This wooden-fenced maze doesn't muck about. Expect to spend up to forty-five minutes finding your way out (or take advantage of the thoughtful emergency exits)

4. Tasmazia & The Village of Lower Crackpot, Tasmania: This delightfully quirky eight-maze destination comes with a handcrafted model town. Discover more on page 216

5. Amaze'n Margaret River, Western Australia: With three-metre-high hedges, the large maze is surrounded by five smaller versions, offering a maze for kids of every age

PENINSULA HOT SPRINGS

Get soaked

 Age minimum: None, but young kids are restricted to the Bath House area after 10am, and kids under sixteen aren't allowed in the Spa Dreaming Centre

 Open: Year round

 Visit: www.peninsulahotsprings.com

The thought of visiting the country's best hot springs with kids in tow might seem as counterintuitive as playing brutal death metal as a soundtrack for meditation.

Even in the presence of therapeutic mineral water, young kids and blissful relaxation don't generally mix. Fortunately, Australia's best hot springs destination is family-friendly, provided your kids respect the spirit of the tranquil outdoor pools. This means it's not a public swimming pool where kids can make water bombs and go berserk.

There is, however, a dedicated kids' area in the Bath House, and kids are allowed to use any of the pools in the main area before 10am, including the hilltop pool with its 360-degree view of the scenic Mornington Peninsula. My kids were more than happy to

Five More Hot Springs for the Family

1. Bitter Springs, Mataranka, Northern Territory

2. Moree Artesian Aquatic Centre, Moree, New South Wales

3. Dalhousie Springs, Witjira National Park, SA

4. Blue Mountains Sparadise Japanese Bath House, Blue Mountains, New South Wales

5. Hastings Caves and Thermal Springs, Hastings, Tasmania

spend time in the kids' area with its shallow waters, shade sail, barrel-bucket soaks and rocky perches to shower beneath fresh-piped water.

At these temperatures, kids can stay in water forever, potty time notwithstanding. As with toys, kids love variety, and with so much to explore, they won't keep in one place for too long. Hey, if you wanted to truly relax, you should probably have left the kids at home and booked a very long, very quiet and very excellent vine-leaf massage in the adjacent Spa Dreaming Centre – no kids allowed.

Close to the Bath House, the

Reflexology Walk consists of a shallow underwater pathway with differently sized pebbles underfoot to stimulate mind and body. Your kids won't buy it, so you'll probably have to carry them, adding extra weight, pressure and presumably, more benefits.

Be advised that kids shouldn't soak too long in any hot spring without frequent water breaks. Nor should they spend much time in Underground Saunas or steaming Turkish hamams. Don't worry, the staff will remind of you of this fact about eleven seconds after you take children into one.

More success might be found in the Cave Pool and Massaging Showers, but good luck with the Cold Plunge. Given the hushed tones and overall serenity of the place, your kids will quickly realise that Peninsula Hot Springs is an altogether different kind of water-park, and will likely want to return to the Bath House where their yelps are splashes are more acceptable.

At this point, I suggest the adults divide and conquer, one staying with the kids while the other revisits the most peaceful pools to soak in the outdoor tran-quillity of this fabulously designed spa. Peninsula Hot Springs is the vision of two local brothers, and so

the concept of family is built into the experience. The kids will have a blast, and eventually, you might get a chance to relax after all.

PHILLIP ISLAND

A feature of creatures

 Age minimum: None

 Open: Year round

 Visit: www.visitphillipisland.com

Young kids are wired to love animals. From books and stuffed toys to nursery rhymes, we're more than happy to act as Old MacDonald on their imaginary farms. My son Galileo's first words were 'E-I-E-I-O' which he used to describe all animals in general.

The result is that any destination promising horses, cows, ducks, dogs and sheep – never mind koalas, kangaroos and penguins – gets toddlers fired up. Phillip Island is located 140 kilometres south-east of Melbourne, connected to the mainland by bridge and known for its scenic coastline, fantastic surfing, motor racing Grand Prix Circuit, wildlife ecotours and nightly Penguin Parade.

Driving down from Melbourne for a day trip, we kicked things off at the Koala Conservation Centre,

where the kids had their first encounter with Australia's most iconic little marsupial. Relaxed in their double pram on the raised boardwalk, it didn't take the kids long to spot their first koala, munching eucalyptus leaves in the nook of a tree, unperturbed by a dozen tourists taking photos.

We spotted a few more along the 600-metre Tree Top Woodland Boardwalk, including one so close that Raquel wanted to reach out and hug him. Once the kids realised that koalas are prone to basically just sit around and munch leaves all day (speaking of which, a single leaf can take ten days to digest), they became more interested in picking their own fragrant eucalyptus leaves and keeping lookout for copperhead snakes.

Next we visited the Churchill Island Heritage Farm to see sheep-shearing, whip-cracking and working dog demonstrations. I was given the opportunity to literally crack the whip, which I did more successfully than another dad, who managed to crack the whip in his eyeball. It's not quite as easy as Indiana Jones makes it look. The presentations and the idyllic setting kept the kids engaged.

A half-hour's drive away is the
Nobbies Centre on Phillip Island's
westernmost tip. Here, the stunning
coastline lives up to its reputation,

with the modern visitor centre
offering sweeping views of the ocean,
further accessed by a long boardwalk
outside. You'll also find hot meals, a
gift shop, and an unusual augmented
reality exhibit about Antarctica.

We holed up with busloads
of tourists to wait for the island's
premier event: the nightly march of
the penguins, the Penguin Parade.
Watching hundreds of the world's
smallest penguin – the little or fairy
penguin – emerge from the ocean
each sunset is one of the most
popular attractions in the entire
country.

There are various viewing
platforms and lookout posts to
choose from. We signed up for the

several thousand flashes, unlike say, the eyes of local Phillip Islander Chris Hemsworth.

The penguin action kicks off just before dark, which can be quite late in the summer months. There's something about these tiny waddling birds that drives tourists crazy. A long day without napping had driven our kids crazy already. Just as the penguins finally emerged, the kids both went into meltdown mode. Packing so much into one day was a tad ambitious – I suggest you spend a couple of days on the island and plan for the Penguin Parade to be a later night than usual, and you'll be singing 'E-I-E-I-O' all the way home.

Penguins Plus platform, which is limited to 300 people, overlooks the most popular pathway, and includes ranger commentary. No photography is allowed during the Penguin Parade because penguin eyes have not evolved to deal with

PUFFING BILLY

Full steam ahead

 Age minimum: None, but folding or narrow-type pushers are the only prams that can fit on the train

 Open: Year round, closed on Christmas Day

 Visit: www.puffingbilly.com.au

CENTRAL DEBORAH GOLD MINE

Go deep

 Age minimum: Three years. Visitors aged between three and fifteen years must be accompanied by an adult

 Open: Year round, closed Christmas Day

 Visit: www.central-deborah.com

An hour and a half north of Melbourne, Bendigo is a quiet city with a rich history still evident in its Victorian–era buildings and downtown tramway. I say 'rich' because Bendigo was once one of the wealthiest cities in the world, sitting at the forefront of the biggest gold rush in history.

Gold was first discovered in the region in 1851 on an unassuming sheep farm, and within a year, tens of thousands of prospectors had flooded in, along with all the people required to service them. Once the rivers were panned out, Californian gold miners recognised that conditions were ripe for an underground reef, and miners began blasting tunnels ever deeper into the earth.

One such mine was Central Deborah, which continues to operate as it did a century ago, albeit with a different purpose. Instead of gold, which has become too expensive to extract, Central Deborah 'mines' experiences, offering a variety of hands-on excursions to introduce visitors to the conditions and mechanics of a working Victorian gold mine.

Provided with overalls, a hard hat and miner's lamp, we signed up my daughter for the seventy-five-minute tour to Level 2, sixty-one metres underground. There are levels and experiences for kids of all ages, ranging from the 3+ Mine Experience and 8+ Underground Adventure to the 14+ Nine Levels of Darkness, accessed via a crammed, manually operated mine lift that takes you 228 metres below the surface. This one might not suit the claustrophobic, but the entry-level tour has plenty to offer little ones, including an industrial lift, which is a lot more comfortable (and presumably safer) than the century-old sardine box miners once used.

We were guided into a series of dark tunnels, learning how miners did their job in such a harsh environment, encountering various machines and a vein of gold still in the bedrock. If your kid wants to know why gold is so valuable, given its few practical uses, tell them that many adults are still trying to figure that one out.

Parents will enjoy the history, kids will enjoy dressing up for a dark, lamp-lit adventure and both will enjoy returning to the surface for a miner's pastie, filled with meat, veg and baked apple. The thick pastry crust enabled miners to eat the tasty filling without having to wash their dusty, grease-caked and possibly arsenic-tainted hands.

Back on the surface, you can explore the old Blacksmith's Shop, the Carbide Lamp Room and the Engine Room, with the only working winder still in use in the entire country. There's a replica of the 27.2-kilogram Hand of Faith nugget found in the area, and kids can also pan for gold.

Beyond the mine, spend some time wandering about Bendigo, checking out Chancery Lane, Rosalind Park, the Golden Dragon Museum & Chinese Garden and the visitor centre. You can also take the kids for a ride on the historic Bendigo tramway, recalling the boom time when the wealth of the world was mined out of central Victoria.

FAIRY PARK

Once upon a time

 Age minimum: None. Fully paved paths make it easy to navigate with prams, although some sections are steep

 Open: Friday to Monday, all school holidays and public holidays except for Christmas Day

 Visit: www.fairypark.com

Once upon a time, a German immigrant family decided to turn their passion for crafting model characters into a park for all to enjoy – and everyone lived happily ever after. Goldilocks and the Three Bears, Snow White, Little Red Riding Hood, Cinderella... you don't have to travel to Disneyland to meet the world's most iconic fairytale stars (and who says Disney should dominate these classics, anyway?).

Opened in 1959, Fairy Park was Australia's first themed attraction, and has maintained its painstaking devotion to the magic of fairytales, elves, dragons and castles ever

since. About an hour's drive from Melbourne, the park features three themed areas, built on a hill and spread over twenty-two acres of landscaped gardens.

Fairytale Land gathers the best of the Brothers Grimm and other European fables into lifelike displays, nearly two-dozen of which come alive with movement, sound and lighting at the push of a button.

The Camelot Adventure Playground celebrates knights, maidens, dragons, princesses, giant toadstools and chivalry, firing up the imagination as young kids scramble through tunnels and

climb up towers. A large model train circles the hilltop castle, a miniature glimpse into a European wonderland, while views of the Mount Anakie are on full display from King Arthur's Rock.

The kitsch visuals and decades of wear are evident, and some visitors have complained online that Fairy Park no longer delivers the magic of their childhood memories. Of course not, you nitwits!

This is a place designed to engage the imaginations and dreams of young kids, not adults visiting two decades later. Preschoolers don't see scuff marks, just their favourite stories coming to life and the chance to play in a

setting they've only seen in book illustrations and, yes, Disney movies.

Personally, we appreciated Fairy Park's lack of Disney's

hyper-consumerism and, even more so, the difference in the ticket price. (Especially if your two year old does what ours did, and spends half an hour dancing to *Puff the Magic Dragon*.)

Spending two to three hours in the company of the kids' favourite characters is priceless for them. If you're local, dress them up in their favourite fairy/princess/knight/ hero costume for extra oomph.

Hot food is available as well, or you can take advantage of various picnic facilities, including barbecue hot plates.

THE GREAT OCEAN ROAD

Road trip

 Age minimum: None

 Open: Year round

 Visit: www.visitgreatoceanroad.org.au

Australia's most iconic coastal drive is also the world's largest war memorial, and it's no battle to see why it's a sweet little road trip for the kids. The full touring route spans 664 kilometres from Geelong to the fishing village of Port Fairy. The goal is to take your time, to spend a week or two exploring the lovely coastal towns and natural attractions along the way.

This is exactly what we *didn't* do, not by choice, but by logistical necessity. I'll save you the rushed, long and winding drive that took us from Melbourne all the way to Adelaide in a couple of days, and reveal instead how we should have done it. Firstly, if at all possible, avoid the week around Christmas and New Year.

We departed on New Year's Day and ran into formidable traffic in Anglesea, Lorne and Apollo Bay, which would have been fine if we were spending a night or two in any of these places instead of trying to find a pie shop (easy) and parking for our vehicle and trailer (not so much).

We'd been warned that the winding coastal road plays hard rock drums inside toddlers' tummies, especially those prone to carsickness. Thwarting the inevitable backseat puke fiasco, we dosed them

up (I know, #ParentsoftheYear, what can we say?) and they promptly fell asleep for the flat highway driving, and woke up understandably groggy and irritable when we got to the curvy bits.

There was no vomit, but that might have been preferable to driving the Great Ocean Road with two pissed-off toddlers. Point is, if you're worried about puke, time your travel sickness meds so they kick in when you need it.

Although the road can be narrow, there are convenient pull-outs to take in the view and get photos, and spots to park so you can explore some of the beautiful beaches you'll pass along the way. Torquay, Fairhaven, Anglesea, Port Campbell – prepare for plenty of beach action, and if the weather isn't playing ball, bundle up for walks in the great ocean breeze.

Whether you're exploring rock pools, hunting for shells, watching the surf or running about like lunatics, the windswept and isolated beaches are special. The towns themselves offer more than just places to stop for meals. Torquay's Surf World is Australia's national surf museum, a worthy visit for those into surfing or needing something to do when the pros aren't nailing waves on the legendary Bells Beach.

Great Otway National Park is a highlight, with its Cape Otway light station, rusted ship-wrecks, dense fern-filled forest, canopy walkways and Otway Fly Adventures ziplines. In a journey of scenic highlights, the star attraction is undoubtedly the Twelve Apostles, consisting of eight large limestone sentinels guarding the steep southern cliffs. There's a sizeable trailer-friendly parking lot, with trails to various viewing points. Bundle up for bracing and biting winds, even in summer.

Further along is the lookout and beach trail for Loch Ard Gorge. There, the limestone glows in the late afternoon sun through to dusk, so staying somewhere like Port Campbell is a good idea (we found a great Airbnb further inland in Timboon).

Continue onward to Warrnambool and the historic fishing village of Port Fairy, where the Great Ocean Road Touring Route officially ends. As with all family travel, taking your time equals time well spent, and while some attractions like the Twelve Apostles are must-sees, this is one experience where you'll have more success focusing on the journey, not the destination.

WHERE TO STAY

Congratulations! You've chosen your destination, and figured out your transport and timing. Now, you have to choose a place to stay, which can make or break your trip.

Depending on your situation at home, you've probably realised the unique challenges of co-sleeping, sharing a room with kids, kids sharing a room with each other and having kids in the first place.

No matter how many activities surround the destination, your choice of accommodation is no longer *just a place to park your head*, as it was in your pre-kid era.

There are all sorts of factors at play, and after staying with my kids in more than fifty hotels, apartment rentals, holiday parks and Airbnbs in just six months, rest assured that I've considered them for you.

As with most decisions in life, there are always pros and cons. One thing I will note: I met dozens of parents travelling with young kids for lengthy periods of time, and a common grumble was that we had all believed our kids would quickly adapt on the road and find a travel rhythm. Unfortunately reality hadn't lived up to our optimistic fantasies. Like so many adults, kids tend to embrace routine, and struggle with change.

They do adapt eventually, in a way, but it takes much *longer* than anyone anticipates, and it doesn't happen nearly as effortlessly as you'll delude yourself into believing. This basically sums up parenting.

where do we stay?

where do we stay **hotels**
where do we stay **holiday parks**
where do we stay **apartment rentals**
where do we stay **air bnb**
where do we stay **motels**
where do we stay **backpackers**
where do we stay **caravans**
where do we stay **motorhomes**
where do we stay **friends and family**

Search   I'm Feeling Lucky

APARTMENT RENTALS

Apartment rentals gave us the closest approximation to the comfort of home, including a small living room, laundry, a dining area and, most importantly, a kitchen to make meals.

This not only saves money on eating out all the time, but it can also

allow for 11pm meltdowns to be salvaged with smashed avocado toast (for kids and parents alike).

Having two or more bedrooms creates separate spaces, and grants some much-needed parenting downtime. Rooms are serviced with towels and toiletries when needed, but there's no daily room service – a positive, as I've found room service often creates the stress of having to clean up *for* the cleaners (after all, we can't let them in with this mess!).

We stayed in a dozen Oaks Hotels properties in major and secondary urban markets (as well as a few resort destinations) and the location was always central, offered useful amenities like swimming pools and was close to restaurants and supermakets.

HOLIDAY PARKS

Cabins in holiday parks offer the same advantages as apartment rentals, with the valuable addition of playgrounds, jumping pillows, gardens and, more importantly, other kids for yours to play with.

We stayed at Discovery Holiday Parks, finding cabins that ranged from the large and modern (Perth, Barossa Valley) to rustic and homey (Cradle Mountain, Airlie Beach) and various iterations in between.

Beyond having your own kitchen, there are communal barbecues and picnic areas, waterparks, play-grounds, rental bikes and other onsite activities to entertain the kids. We were particularly fond of the social vibe we found in Discovery Holiday Parks.

We connected with many parents travelling with toddlers, whether they were in motorhomes or cars, camping or, like us, staying in cabins. Unlike hotels or apartment rentals, holiday parks encourage a positive and social environment for both kids and parents.

CARAVANS

Taking on the Big Lap with kids is increasingly popular, and customising or purchasing a specialised motorhome or caravan is one way to go about it.

The biggest pro – beyond affordability, depending on how long your trip is – is the opportunity to build familiarity and routine into your travels.

Young kids thrive on consistency, although many a parent we met alerted us to other challenges, including sleeping in a small space (effectively co-sleeping), living in a small space, mechanical issues, emptying the blackwater and battling clutter, among others.

Caravans and motorhomes can be a serious endeavour – one couple we

met designed their caravan with absurd attention to detail and amazing space-saving tricks – but a rental can also be a simple option for extended holidays.

I recommend renting a motorhome first and doing a trial run to see whether it fits your personality and family dynamic.

AIRBNB AND HOLIDAY RENTALS

We became big fans of Airbnb on our Australian trip, and stayed in more than a dozen properties around the country. Typically, we searched for family-friendly homes that came pre-loaded with toys, books, play areas, kids' utensils, cribs and a layout devoid of sharp edges and antique vases.

When it worked – as it did in Lennox Head, Melbourne, Geraldton, Timboon and Hobart – it was fantastic. The kids were happy (other kids' toys!), we could relax, plus, we got a voyeuristic glimpse into other people's lives, and even learned parenting tips along the way (we never thought the kids would take to a chalkboard so well!).

Reading reviews and doing research about the area is crucial to the success of the platform, as is communicating with your hosts. The value for money is definitely there, and we took pains to look after people's stuff, as we hoped they would look after ours (indeed, we were renting our own home on Airbnb to families with young kids back in Canada). Simply put, the share economy works, until it doesn't.

THE AIRBNB INCIDENT

Although Airbnb fully delivered on the platform's promise nine out of ten times, it's worth mentioning the one time it didn't.

In Bangkok, we booked a house and arranged an airport pick-up with the owner. When we got to the property, we discovered a) he had lied about the location, b) he had lied about its amenities and c) he had lied about his profile (he was in fact a she).

The place was a death trap for young kids. There was a leaking water pump, no safety rails on the stairs, bugs everywhere and a burned-out stovetop with broken kitchen appliances. The actual location was an industrial zone, located miles from anywhere, with no street lighting and lots of stray dogs. The 'beach' nearby consisted of concrete rocks covered in rubbish.

We called Airbnb immediately and complained. They told us to find somewhere else and we would get a refund. Safety, they assured us, was their number one priority. It took us hours just to get a taxi out of there, and a few days in a fleabag hotel before we found another Airbnb that was 1000 per cent better for about one third more of the price.

Then, Airbnb told us they'd conducted an investigation and, because of their strict cancellation policy, they wouldn't refund us anything. In other words, we paid for a two-week stay in a place we stayed in for a total of three hours (and two of those were spent trying to leave).

We complained furiously, but it turns out Airbnb tend to side with property owners who bring in regular revenue over guests, especially in this case, as the property owner represented several properties. Airbnb insisted the owner would fix the location info and amenities, and we had no further recourse other than writing a scathing review. I also discovered that if we made too much of a stink of it, Airbnb might yank our own property off their system, a big risk since we were dependent on our own Airbnb rental income for our trip.

The entire situation is technically known in the consumer complaints world as a Complete Crock of Horseshit. That being said, the rest of our Airbnb experiences were overwhelmingly positive.

Should you find yourself in a property that resembles our Bangkok disaster, take as many photos as you can as evidence (we took a few, but it turns out not enough) and get the name and number of everyone you speak to at Airbnb.

The entire experience left us in little doubt that *profit*, not safety, is Airbnb's number one priority.

HOTELS AND MOTELS

As a young kid, my parents would take us on family holidays to a hotel resort in a small beach town. I loved the smell of the just-vacuumed hallways. I loved the smell of the just-vacuumed rooms. The endless towels, the free movie channel, the buffet breakfast, the daily activities for kids: pillow fights! Ping-pong tournaments! Water polo!

It instilled in me a love for all hotels, which might explain why I ended up becoming a travel writer.

But these memories were formed when I was old enough to remember them. Before that, I've been told, we stayed in vacation rental-type homes, because sharing a hotel room with young kids is like sharing a crib with young kids; they're on top of you twenty-four seven, and there's nowhere to hide.

In hotels, my wife and I have actually had to hide inside a wardrobe for a glass of wine, and, *ahem*, conjugal visit. If you're *lucky* to have kids who are old enough, you can get them their own room.

Some hotels have adjoining rooms, which is a useful option. Some resorts have kitchens or kitchenettes, with the same advantages of an apartment rental. In your basic hotel room, however, the lack of a kitchen and space is troublesome. The minibar fridge can quickly become inadequate, and, after a long day dealing with the kids, expensive! Without a nappy bin, it also becomes odorous pretty fast.

We stayed in a few traditional hotel rooms on our trip, including one that was a converted shipping container. Sometimes we had fun, but we never got much sleep. If you've got a baby or toddler and are not travelling with a portable cot, always request one ahead of time to get the little one out of your bed and to give your zeds a fighting chance.

SLEEPING ARRANGEMENTS

Sleeping with a young kid is like sharing your bed with a drunken octopus looking for its car keys. In our case, we had two. Consider our options:

Both parents and kids in one bed.

One parent on the couch, both kids in bed with the other parent.

One kid in one bed, both parents and the other kid (who spins like the hands of a clock) in the other.

One or both kids on the floor by the bed.

Both parents on the couch, kids in the bed.

One parent in the bathtub (this actually happened).

One kid with one parent in one of the bed/bedrooms, the other with the other.

Kids both asleep in their own beds, parents in their own bed ... ha, as if.

It's crucial to recognise the three-hour time delay between 'putting the kids to bed' and your kids *actually* sleeping.

I remember taking my daughter camping with a mate and his young daughter. The plan was to put the kids to bed in the tents, and then meet for a cold beer around the fire. Once we entered our respective tents, we never emerged.

Perhaps you have kids that will sleep anywhere. Perhaps you have kids that sleep through the whole night. Perhaps you have kids that fall asleep by themselves without having their backs/arms/hair massaged. Lucky you.

When it comes to bedtime on the road, many kids will be a little rattled by the change of environment, because many kids are rattled even if the environment is exactly the same. I beg my kids to sleep. I sing them

to sleep. I massage them, coo to them, recite spells, blessings and inevitably, curses. I endure their thirty-five nightly excuses, delays and stalls,
including but not limited to the following classics, always prefaced with:
'But Dad, but Dad, but Dad...'

1.   My pyjamas are too big!

2.   My pyjamas are too small!

3.   I'm too hot!

4.   I'm too cold!

5.   It's too light in here!

6.   It's too dark in here!

7.   This bed is too soft!

8.   This bed is too hard!

9.   I need a gummy worm!

10. My knuckles hurt!

11. The shadow looks like a monster!

12. I need another hug!

13. Just two/four/six/twenty more minutes, I promise!

14. I want to hear *What Does the Fox Say*!

15. Something smells funny!

16. Your eyes look red and runny!

17. It's not fair!

18. My nose hurts!

19. My pyjamas are bugging me!

20. I want to pee!

21. I want to poo!

22. I want a haircut!

23. The snow monster in *Frozen* gives me nightmares!

24. The volcano monster in *Moana* gives me nightmares!

25. My stuffed toy is dirty!

26. My feet are hot!

27. My feet are cold!

28. I don't like these socks!

29. My brother is still awake!

30. I want cereal!

31. Just one more story, I promise!

32. I'm too excited from today!

33. I'm too excited for tomorrow!

34. I have too much energy!

35. I just want to sleep with you guys!

To be fair, my daughter, Raquel, unleashes all these excuses on most nights, whether we travel or not.

She just *hates* sleeping, until it's time to get up in the morning, at which time, Raquel *loves* sleeping.

SOUTH

AUSTRALIA

OCEANIC VICTOR

Sandwiched by tuna

 Age minimum: None. Younger kids will probably be freaked out by the size of the tuna, but will still enjoy the experience

 Open: Year round

 Visit: www.oceanicvictor.com.au

In Victor Harbour, about ninety minutes' drive from Adelaide, the Oceanic Victor is an in-sea aquarium that puts your family among the fish, and one impressive fish in particular.

Southern bluefin tuna weigh up to 200 kilograms and blitz about the oceans at speeds up to seventy kilometres an hour. Port Lincoln has developed a hugely successful tuna-ranching industry, breeding highly prized tuna sustainably in large netted enclosures. A similar enclosure was transported to Victor Harbour, and has become a unique educational facility for adults and kids, allowing us to interact with and learn all about the Ferrari of the oceans.

Founder Yasmin Stehr told me she was inspired by how kids reacted to tuna encounters at the ranch pens in Port Lincoln, and thought she could do one better closer to the big city. We arrived at Oceanic Victor's launch in Granite Island, ready to take the boat ride just a few minutes offshore to the circular pen.

Marine biologists operate the facility, ensuring both tuna and humans are in great hands. We hopped on board and could see the dark shadows of about eighty tuna swimming in the turquoise ocean.

A separate pool is home to a friendly Port Jackson shark and schools of other fish, while a touch pool holds starfish, mussels and anemone, delighting my two year old who could finally look *and* touch.

Although warm out, we were provided with wetsuits, snorkels and masks for an additional layer of warmth and protection. I took the hand of my four year old as we entered the tuna pen. Although it's perfectly safe, the sight of a very large fish swimming with you in a rather small pool would unnerve most adults. That is, if you manage to spot more than a dark shadow . . . the tuna are so fast and agile they appear ethereal.

Since my daughter was smaller than some of the fish around us, I can't blame her for wanting to get the hell out of the pool – like, *now*! I was just proud that she got

into the water in the first place. Not to worry, one of the staff invited my daughter over to grab some sardines and throw them in the water all around me. Water exploded as tuna swooped in for their lunch. Given their size and speed, I was grateful that humans don't feature on *their* menu.

One of the marine biologists handed my daughter a pole with a sardine attached at the end. She held it over the water and within seconds a tuna launched through the surface to snatch its meal. The result was squeals of delight from the kids, and the customary pleas for more.

Fortunately, there were a lot of tuna to be fed, and they needed a lot more sardines to feed them. Watching the kids' excitement while sandwiched by tuna splashing around me is one of the most enduring memories of my Australian adventure.

Next I hopped into the adjacent pool to meet the big-lipped Port Jackson shark, diving underwater to wave to my elated kids, who viewed the action from an underwater observatory. We showered off and returned to land, catching the Clydesdale horse–drawn tram ferry along the 630-metre-long causeway back to the car park. It had been an exhilarating and unforgettable day in the company of one of the ocean's most extraordinary fish.

KANGAROO ISLAND

Not the Galapagos

 Age minimum: None

 Open: Year round

 Visit: www.tourkangarooisland.com.au

five year old on your shoulders. Advised by an enthusiastic guide to stick together on the beach, my daughter had more fun running on the 900-metre wooden boardwalk, and peering at sea lions waddling to the shoreline below.

We crossed the island to our next destination, the Kangaroo Island Wilderness Retreat, located just outside Flinders Chase National Park. Wallabies wandered about the grounds, delighting the kids, as did a night-time walk searching for koalas in the trees. The staff naturalist was a big-hearted chap named Nature, a fitting moniker for a fine ambassador for the island's wildlife.

Things are very well named on Kangaroo Island. Take the 500-million-year-old Remarkable Rocks in Flinders Chase. Scrambling with the kids around, under and inside these geological marvels was the highlight of our KI visit.

All this to say: it's best to adjust your expectations of Kangaroo Island. It is not an unfenced zoo. You'll see animals, sure, but there's so much more. Budget for at least a weekend here, although a relaxed week would be even better.

HAIGH'S CHOCOLATES

Seconds please!

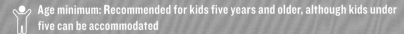 **Age minimum:** Recommended for kids five years and older, although kids under five can be accommodated

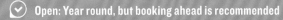 **Open:** Year round, but booking ahead is recommended

 **Visit:** www.haighschocolates.com.au

You had me at 'chocolate factory'. Haigh's is Australia's oldest and best-known chocolatier, founded in downtown Adelaide in 1915.

While its iconic storefront on King William Street is still in operation, take the kids to the factory and visitor centre in the Adelaide suburb of Parkside. I expect little resistance when you proclaim 'It's time to visit a chocolate factory!' – I've never seen my kids get dressed so fast.

I'd highly recommend *not* watching either of the two Willy Wonka movies beforehand, because there will be no Oompa Loompas running about, and it's always best to manage children's expectations.

Rather, you enter through a normal-looking gift shop with a wide variety of chocolates. Free, guided behind-the-scenes tours run daily, kicking off with a debrief in a small room that will likely find you trying to pay attention as your kids squirm and whine. All that cocoa in the air must act as a sort of catnip for young kids.

You'll learn that Haigh's sources its cocoa from Venezuela and Papua New Guinea, and that each of their famous Easter eggs is hand-wrapped. You'll learn about the fascinating process of turning the seed of a tropical plant into a decadent global treat. Founder John Haigh recognised that Australian chocolates were sorely lacking in quality and, determined to do something about it, wrote to

Dark Chocolate Truffle

of activity. We watched machines churn out chockies to be closely inspected and, when they failed the test, watched them be discarded to the discounted seconds pile.

It's all very industrious, as you'd expect, and soon enough you'll be back in the gift shop, where you'll discover the *true* cost of a free factory tour. Our little one attached himself to a lamb stuffed toy, which was attached to a large Easter egg. We raided the seconds pile for the bargain, since we'd just learned that there was absolutely nothing wrong with them, and that fractionally off chocolate cuts don't matter much when you're guzzling them.

Did you know that chocolate naturally releases neurotransmitters like phenylethylamine and serotonin that lift your mood and make you feel happier? It also contains a fat called anadamide, which activates your dopamine receptors, enhancing the feeling of happiness. Eating chocolate also releases endorphins, which decrease levels of stress and pain. Needless to say, parents travelling with young kids might want to schedule more than one visit to a chocolate factory.

the most famous chocolatiers in Switzerland asking for advice.

Surprisingly, Lindt replied, and John Haigh of Adelaide soon found himself apprenticing with the world's best chocolatiers. Four generations later, Haigh's has grown from John's first factory (in his garden) to eighteen stores across four states. All of which means nothing to a five year old chomping at the chewy bit.

So we left the debrief room and gazed through large picture windows at factory workers wrapping, squeezing, mixing, fashioning, inspecting, painting and moulding a variety of chocolates. It was a hive

SILVER SANDS BEACH

Drive slowly

 Age minimum: None

 Open: Year round

 Visit: www.aldingabayonline.com.au

Some readers won't think much of driving on a large, white sandy beach. Depending where you live, this might be something you do all the time. Other readers, like me, will get a huge buzz when steering their car onto the wide, stunning white sands of Sellicks, Silver Sands or Aldinga beaches.

Calm waves lap at your wheels along this six-kilometre stretch, and while it might get busy on public holidays, there's plenty of space to pass slow-going motorists with their windows down, their music cranked and kids hanging out the windows or sunroof, wondering how all this is even possible.

The beaches form part of the Fleurieu Peninsula, a beautiful part of South Australia that is home to McLaren Vale wineries, artisan food markets and fine country living. In the distance, the Mount Lofty Ranges look like an artist

painted them onto the landscape. Depending on which way you're headed, don't miss the sweeping views out across the Great Australian Bight.

Of course, we had to stop the car on the beach to have a splash around, facing west for a post-card-perfect sunset. This is exactly the kind of place you imagine when you think about 'long walks on the beach'.

There are various access points to drive on the beaches, and condensed sand means you don't need a four-wheel drive. Whether it's part of a beach day, a place to stop while exploring the peninsula or something new to try on your way from Adelaide to Victor Harbour, don't pass up the opportunity to drive on this sparkling-clean beach. Windows down, wind in the hair, big beats – even if it's the goddamn Wiggles – cranked to the max.

Final tip: you may want to pass up the more expensive local restaurants with the kids in tow, but definitely pop into Aldinga Bay Café for some unexpectedly fine Indian food.

MONARTO ZOO'S LIONS 360

Hear them roar

 Age minimum: None

 Open: Year round

 Visit: www.monartozoo.com.au/lions360

Here's a unique animal encounter with just the right amount of thrill to inspire kids to care about one of nature's great animals. In the 1970s, a survivor of a great white shark attack visited the lion enclosure in Adelaide Zoo.

It inspired him to pioneer a special cage to observe and learn about the marine predator that almost took his life. Now, nearly half a century later, shark cage diving has inspired Australia's first lion cage encounter; talk about coming full circle.

An hour outside Adelaide, the Lions 360 experience in Monarto Zoo places you inside the cage as hungry lions gather all around. Driving from Adelaide, the scenery reminded me of the African savanna, and indeed, the similar climate and conditions have allowed Monarto to successfully introduce an African animal-breeding program.

This is why Australia's largest open-range zoo is home to giraffes, zebras, antelopes, white rhinos, cheetahs and hyenas in large enclosures accessible only by guided bus tours. My daughter and I first checked out the chimpanzees, which were particularly active that

MONARTO ZOO'S LIONS 360

recent extinction of the northern white rhino.

Over the past twenty-one years, poachers and habitat encroachment have wiped out some 43 per cent of Africa's wild lion population, and their numbers continue to decline. As a conservation organisation, Monarto is part of an international lion-breeding program, with three adult males and eight adult females. The males are housed separately from the females, and it's the lionesses that steal the show at Lions 360.

The Lions 360 experience is offered twice a day during feeding time. Our bus arrived at an enclosure with the lions already gathered. We entered through a door, walked along a tunnel and there they were: standing on hind legs, prowling up and down, two on top of the cage right above us. Carefully monitoring the food allocation, the conservation officer briefed us on their behaviour and began to feed the big cats with his metal tongs.

'Don't get your hands too close to the cage; they'd love to add them to their lunch!' he said. This is not your typical zoo experience: the pride is engaged and curious, and

morning, especially one of the little baby chimps fooling around on monkey bars.

'It's an ape, not too different from us,' I told my awed daughter, who learned lots of new things that morning. Education is key to the entire facility. Monarto's breeding programs and support for conservation efforts in Africa are also particularly poignant, given the close enough for us to feel their breath, hear their grunts and smell their musk. With their sharp teeth and claws, and powerful muscles, they truly are fearsome beasts, and even though the cage was perfectly safe, it was hard not to feel that primal fear that makes you want to be anywhere else as long as it's not so close to the hungry lions!

A model Land Rover poked through a section of the cage to give us a close-up glimpse of the lions outside, and to recreate what it feels like to be on safari. A large lioness stood on the vehicle's roof, paying particular attention to some of the young kids in our group. My five-year-old daughter must have looked especially delicious, because a lioness growled loudly right above her head. She held me extra tightly after that.

The sound of a fully grown lion this close was like standing next to a jet engine or an erupting volcano: every cell in your body urges you to book it!

Satiated with their feed, the big cats quickly lost interest in us and wound down. We returned to the bus for a drive through the animal enclosures, the gates of which reminded me very much of Jurassic Park.

Having previously ticked off shark cage diving, I was initially sceptical that a lion cage experience would measure up. Yet Lions 360 proved to be a fascinating experience for all ages. Isn't it about time we took our place inside the cage?

ADELAIDE CENTRAL MARKET

Yummy ants!

 Age minimum: None

 Open: Year round

 Visit: www.ausfoodtours.com

When Cheryl Turner took Raquel's hand on one side and Gali's on the other, I knew things would be just fine. When you do activities with young kids, you never know how different guides will deal with them. We've had experiences where guides treated the young kids like they were annoying disturbances, which, granted, they were, but that's not their fault.

If guides don't have much experience with children, it becomes painfully obvious with every judgemental glare. Other guides, typically those with children themselves, delight in the unbridled enthusiasm that kids bring to the table.

Cheryl works for a company called Food Tours Australia, and she's our guide through the colourful hallways that make up the Adelaide Central Market. It's a busy place with a *lot* of visual and fragrant stimulation. The fact that Cheryl took the kids with grandma-like authority immediately took the pressure off us, so we could enjoy our sensory discovery of South Australia's culinary wonders.

The Central Market is one of the largest covered markets in the southern hemisphere, and draws in more than eight million visitors each year. As one of the city's biggest

attractions, a lot of thought and care goes into what items the stalls can offer. No major brand names or chains stores here, just farm-to-table producers, fresh fruit and vegetables, gourmet condiments, confectionaries, seafood, beverages, snacks and myriad other yummy foodstuffs that will make you wish you had more luggage space and had travelled with a refrigerator.

Cheryl guided us to her favourite farm stalls, where the kids had their 'best plum ever!' and 'best tomato ever!' and best whatever-else-they-put-in-their-mouth ever! We sampled yoghurt, strawberries covered in chocolate, creamy tastebud-tingling cheese, and grapes that tasted distinctly like lychees.

There was fresh roasted coffee for the adults and decadent hot chocolate for the kids. Our highlight was a stall called Something Wild, Australia's first Indigenous greens and game wholesaler. Cheryl handed us a tray of smoked crocodile, emu mettwurst, pepper berry venison and smoked red gum kangaroo.

To my surprise, Raquel was game to try the meats, which, for the most part, tasted like chicken. We also tried quandong, bush apples and karkalla, outback fare rich in health benefits and unique flavours. Quandong, we learned, has more vitamin C than an orange!

As for the strange, green nutty stuff in the white bowl, when we learned these specimens were in fact lemony biting ants from the Northern Territory, it proved a creepy-crawly too far for our brave culinary adventurer.

Now that we had the lay of the land, we loaded up on our favour-ites for a picnic that afternoon, leaving the market with full bellies and a full appreciation for guides who know how to engage with curious, hungry kids.

CLELAND WILDLIFE PARK

Make nice with the roo

 Age minimum: None

 Open: Year round, closed Christmas Day

 Visit: www.clelandwildlifepark.sa.gov.au

Australia has no shortage of wildlife parks. Three are featured in this book, and many more could be.

Back where I live in Canada, it's impossible to take my kids anywhere to feed a kangaroo, pet a koala or pose with a wombat. Not only because I'm on the wrong continent, but also because Canada's native creatures don't take kindly to the attention of toddlers. Not counting Justin Bieber, of course.

Pat a beaver and it will slap its hard, broad tail across your face. Wolverines, moose, bears, elk and grumpy Canadian geese are not animals you'd want to get too close to, much less chase around a large fenced-in enclosure ,which is exactly what my daughter was doing at Cleland Wildlife Park.

She was learning the important lesson that wallabies can hot-foot it very quickly unless you have food, in which case, they will coyly flash their long eyelashes and come right over. The emus are far scarier looking, so we gave them a wide berth.

Part of a ten-square-kilometre conservation area, Cleland's natural bush setting is home to more than 130 species of Australian wildlife. The roos and wallabies have large spaces to roam, and thanks to the park's emphasis on conservation, there are roomy enclosures for

dingoes, devils, bettongs, potoroos, koalas, a large reptile facility and an abundance of native, water and forest birds.

My daughter nervously approached a rather muscular male kangaroo lazing on the ground with the demeanour of someone recovering from a big night out. With feed in hand, Raquel looked to us for reassurance that this was a safe thing to do. What did we know? I'm from South Africa, Mum is from Brazil, and we all live in Canada. I guessed it was all okay, otherwise small children feeding kangaroos wouldn't be a thing to write about in the first place, would it?

Cleland also offers various experiences, from wombat and reptile encounters to koala holds, keeper presentations and night walks when many of the animals are more active. Located just over twenty minutes' drive from Adelaide, it's one of the better places to get up close with the animals that call Australia home.

THE GARDEN OF UNEARTHLY DELIGHTS

Marching along

 Age minimum: None

 Open: Februay to March

🌐 Visit: www.adelaidefringe.com.au
www.gardenofunearthlydelights.com.au

For thirty-one days each year, Adelaide hosts the world's second-largest arts festival, a vibrant celebration that made me wonder why so many people told me 'not much happens in Adelaide'. Granted, these people mostly lived in Sydney and Melbourne, and, quite frankly, they don't know what they're missing.

Mad March brings with it Adelaide Fringe, the world music festival WOMADelaide, Adelaide Festival, Adelaide Writers' Week and the roaring supercars of the Adelaide 500. Sure, the city might cram a lot into just one month, but plenty happens in the City of Churches – certainly more than enough to keep a

travelling family busy.

Staying in the Oaks downtown put us right in the thick of the Fringe action. Buildings along North Terrace became animated backdrops as bright graphics lit up their facades, captivating kids and adults with eccentric themes and Monty Python–esque quirkiness.

Check out the annual program for the kid-friendly performances, or head over on a fine autumn evening to the lively Garden of Unearthly Delights. Easily among the festival's most popular events, Rundle Park transforms into a riot of art, circus performances, gourmet food trucks, buskers, live music, comedy and dance.

With performances scheduled nightly in a variety of different tents, the pop-up carnival with jumping castles and illuminated rides proved popular with our kids, who were juiced up on the stimulation of it all.

A convincing sideshow promoter rebuffed every excuse I could think of as to why I shouldn't bring the kids into a small show tent for a fifteen-minute mime act. With the audience seated in a circle, the mime emerged from behind the curtains with a brilliant act that kept the kids rapt. It all felt authentic and gritty, like the magical travelling circus acts you read about in fantasy novels where anything can happen. *Geek Love*, anyone?

As the city's large fruit bats flapped across the moonlit sky, the bustling garden was full of surprise and wonder – lantern gardens, moving sculptures, fireworks, market stalls and captivating street art.

Even if you don't manage to see any shows at Fringe, make sure you get to the garden and stroll along North Terrace. Despite the opinions of those who don't live in the city, it leaves little doubt that Adelaide has plenty to offer, especially in March.

GLENELG

Just a swell place to be

 Age minimum: None

 Open: Year round

 Visit: www.glenelgsa.com.au

At the end of Adelaide's only tramline rests a lovely beachfront suburb with a Mediterranean-like climate, white sandy beach, lots of restaurants and plenty of activities to keep the kids busy.

Glenelg's fortunes have risen and dipped since the first jetty was unveiled in 1859. It has been home to an aquarium, a shark museum, a Luna Park theme park, a controversial theme park called Magic Mountain, a tea-room kiosk and, more recently, a twenty-five-metre Ferris wheel – all of which have since fallen by the wayside as the waves continue to roll in across the beach. Waves that, reassuringly, haven't changed at all.

Today, summer festivals and events are held alongside the jetty that stretches into Holdfast Bay. Our kids went nuts for the impressive Foreshore Playground, easily one of the best playgrounds in the country. Large slides, pebble pits, mini trampolines, rope play, water features, ramps and tunnels – with so many activity options for the kids, they scarcely noticed the adjacent five-storey Beachouse amusement park.

The 120-year-old merry-go-round is still doing the rounds inside The Beachouse, which also features waterslides, bumper boats, a miniature train and a seven-level play castle for the kids to burn

energy while you replenish yours with a cup of coffee.

Getting little ones to sleep in the stroller is a breeze with a scenic walk along South Esplanade, and later they can splash themselves silly at the fountains in Moseley Square. If you're visiting from the city, you'll definitely want to bring a change of clothes. At the ground level of the striking old Glenelg Town Hall is the Bay Discovery Centre, a social history museum that honours the cultural heritage of the state.

With various exhibitions to keep you busy, the gold-coin donation for entry is well worth it to escape the sun alone.

A hit with the kids, we visited Glenelg several times and never found it overcrowded, unlike some other major urban beachfront promenades. Getting there is a picnic, both by car and tram.

Glenelg left us with the distinct impression that Adelaide deliberately under-markets itself as a great location for young families to live. If it didn't, there'd be traffic jams and line-ups for those trampolines every weekend.

BLUE LAKE AND EWENS PONDS

Freshwater blues

 Age minimum: None

 Open: Year round, but you'll want to visit between December and March (when the Blue Lake is actually blue!)

 Visit: www.reef2ridge.com/snorkelling-tour

Natural attractions are hit and miss with young kids. You can stand beside the world's deepest canyon, highest mountain or widest river, and you're just as likely to get a shrug as a look of wonder.

It's all about context. Without having enough experience to have seen *other* canyons, mountains or rivers, for kids it's just, well, a canyon, mountain or river. Superlatives don't mean much when you have the 'best ice-cream ever', the 'best ride ever' and see the 'best movie ever' every other day.

It's not like the Blue Lake is the world's *bluest* lake, although if someone made the claim I don't know how anyone might prove them otherwise. Each December,

SCUBA DIVING and SNORKELLING are PERMITTED. SWIMMING, FLOATATION DEVICES or WATER CRAFT OF ANY KIND ARE PROHIBITED.

Mount Gambier's Blue Lake is a richer cobalt hue than the glacier lakes of Canada, or the azure salt lakes in the Atacama Desert – my contenders for the world's other bluest lakes.

Located in Mount Gambier itself, the Blue Lake covers the crater of a dormant volcano, and most of the year looks a dullish grey. Certainly not worth driving five hours to see, in any case. Each summer, however, the top layer of the lake heats up, causing molecules of calcium carbonate to scatter blue light waves. This turns the water a car-stopping shade of rich blue, which makes for a truly extraordinary sight.

A 3.6-kilometre walking trail takes you to various lookout points, but since the lake supplies the town with its drinking water, no swimming is permitted. This 'look but don't touch' lake held my daughter's attention for the five minutes I needed to get a photo of the lake holding her attention.

It's a rather unique backdrop for a picnic, which she might even appreciate one day when she's seen a few more lakes, and had a few more picnics. Millennia of geological processes went into creating such a striking natural marvel … and your kids will probably be over it before you've buttered the picnic roll.

Fortunately, time is on your side when it comes to the Ewens Ponds. Twenty-five kilometres from town is a series of three limestone sinkholes that offer one of the best freshwater snorkelling experiences you can have anywhere in the world. There are those superlatives again, although in this case, they're entirely warranted.

Grab your mask and snorkel (or rent a pair from the local Ridge2Reef dive shop) and enter a series of pools with unparalleled visibility. At just nine metres deep, sunshine filters into the ponds to promote rich aquatic life, some of which you can't find anywhere else on the planet. It's like swimming above an underwater botanical garden, or inside an aquarium.

Protected as a conservation area, the water quality is off the charts, but the temperature is a chilly fifteen degrees, so you'll want to rent wetsuits to be comfortable. Go with the flow as you snorkel through narrow channels teeming with plant life, including schools of small blackfish, lampreys, mullet

and common galaxias. You can also wave to the scuba divers below you, enjoying the ponds from a different perspective.

By the time you've crossed the final channel to the third cool pond, you'll be ready to climb up the ladder and into the warm South Australian sunshine. It's a short trudge back to the car park, where it's a good idea to have refreshments waiting. The kids will have sparkles in their eyes, no doubt exclaiming they've just had the 'Best. Swim. Ever!' There's little chance they, or you, will experience anything else like Ewens Ponds in a lifetime.

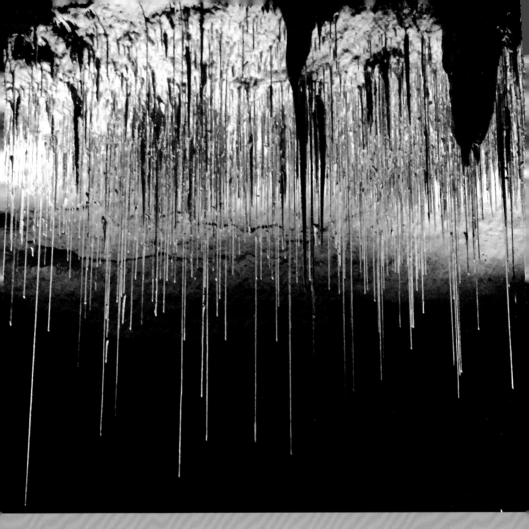

THE NARACOORTE CAVES

A catastrophe for ancient marsupials

 Age minimum: None

 Open: Year round, closed Christmas Day and Catastrophic Fire Days

 Visit: www.naracoortecaves.sa.gov.au

We visit a few show caves in this book, but the ones at Naracoorte Caves National Park are the only Australian caves granted World Heritage status. They are the only caves with giant robotic replicas of ancient wombats on site and are also the only caves we visited the day before a Catastrophic Fire Day.

Having never heard such a term before, it sounded positively apocalyptic – as scary as a ferocious-looking model of a marsupial lion must seem to an eighteen month old who doesn't know it's just a model, and the creature long extinct. South Australia's Bureau of Meteorology calls conditions 'Catastrophic' when it's so hot and dry that a bushfire might break out if someone sneezes too aggressively.

Everything shuts down, and the safest place to be is probably deep in a cool, underground cave, but ironically, the twenty-six caves that make up the Naracoorte cave complex all close on such days. Fortunately, we arrived the day *before* the shutdown, although the thermometer still cracked forty-six degrees.

Like most show caves, Naracoorte boasts impressive stalactites, stalagmites, helictites and soda straw formations. What sets it apart are the sheer number and variety of fossils that have been discovered within, with the caves acting as a sort of pitfall trap for millennia of unsuspecting Australian megafauna.

These fossils, and what they represent, are exhibited in the adjacent Wonambi Fossil Centre, where the kids see replicas and animatronics of the extinct creatures that once roamed these parts.

All was going swimmingly until a sound effect proved too much for our five year old. She jumped into my arms and clutched my neck in a death lock, which put an end to the leisurely part of the experience. The little one didn't mind too much; he quite likes being alone in the dark and is constantly urging us to put him in the trailer and close the doors. This is not only weird; it makes for unsound parenting during a heat wave.

We checked in with the park tours for the Stick-Tomato Cave and the Alexandra Cave. The ambient lighting and the comfortable temperature calmed down Raquel, but sent Gali into hysterics. When you have two young kids, if it's not one, it's the other – and if it's not either, then it's you.

We enjoyed our tour of Alexandra Cave, including the show-stopping mirror-glass Reflecting Pool, where a single drop of water falling from above feels like it ripples the space-time continuum. It's a little disappointing to learn that the Reflecting Pool is actually an artificial creation, constructed by the guy who discovered the caves and hoped to turn them into a tourist attraction.

Job well done, although nature does tend to do a fine job on its own. By the end of our visit, both kids were exhausted and overstimulated, a perfect set-up for a long nap as we continued our blissfully air-conditioned road trip to Kingston SE.

The Big Things

There are over 150 Big Things in Australia, and many more Next Big Things, currently playing on Triple J. The Big Banana in Coffs Harbour is probably the most famous Big Thing in Australia, and for those who are counting, New South Wales has the most Big Things.

I passed at least a dozen of these Things, and I regret not stopping the car to take photos, as opposed to just pointing each Thing out to my kids, who likely had already missed it. I wasn't about to circle back to interrupt whatever peace we might have been experiencing in the car. On the other hand, Big Things come to the rescue during any meltdown when you excitedly point out the car window and say, 'Stop crying and look ... there's a Big Pumpkin !'

Big Things provide towns with a fun and recognisable land-mark. Take Kingston SE's Big Lobster, which stands seven-teen metres tall, weighs four tons, and was built with steel and fibreglass. It's a particularly impressive Big Thing that shadows the highway and was designed to draw attention to a restaurant, which it somehow failed to do.

During our visit, both the restaurant and the Big Lobster had For Sale signs attached. Larry the Lobster (as locals call it) has fallen on hard times since its erection in 1979, but even so, a giant rock lobster is too weird and wonderful to ignore.

Tour buses were parked on the side of the road, and my kids ran around the lobster, burning off some energy before we hit Kingston's real highlights: the white sandy beach and, later, one of the most magical sunsets we saw in the entire country. After all, Big Things are just a little excuse to stop, look around, and discover something new.

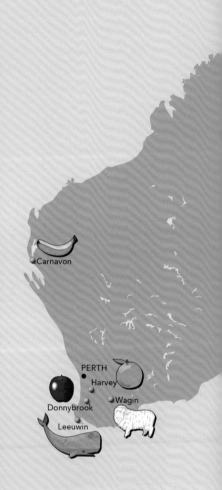

Carnavon

PERTH

Harvey

Wagin

Donnybrook

Leeuwin

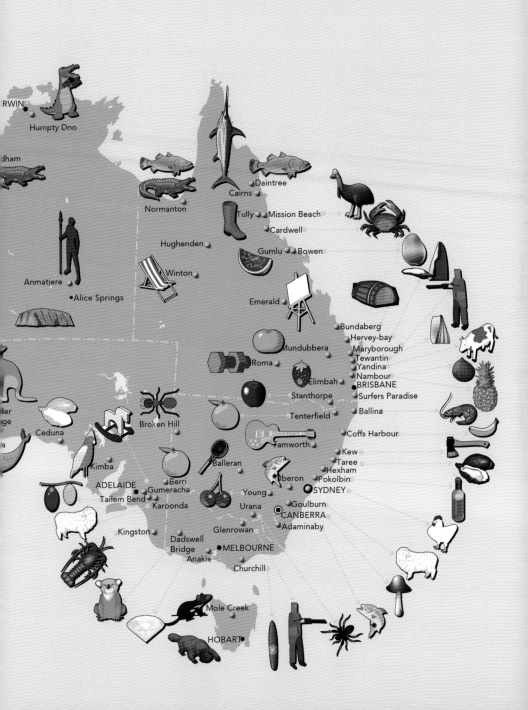

RWIN

Humpty Doo

dham

Anmatjere

•Alice Springs

Normanton

Hughenden

Winton

Cairns

Daintree

Tully

Mission Beach

Cardwell

Gumlu

Bowen

Emerald

Mundubbera

Roma

Elimbah

Stanthorpe

Bundaberg

Hervey-bay

Maryborough

Tewantin

Yandina

Nambour

BRISBANE

Surfers Paradise

Ballina

Tenterfield

Coffs Harbour

Ceduna

Kimba

Broken Hill

ADELAIDE

Gumeracha

Tailem Bend

Karoonda

Berri

Balleran

Young

Urana

Tamworth

Oberon

Kew

Taree

Hexham

Pokolbin

SYDNEY

Goulburn

CANBERRA

Adaminaby

Kingston

Dadswell
Bridge

Anakie

Glenrowan

MELBOURNE

Churchill

Mole Creek

HOBART

PACK LIKE A PRO

The first and most important thing you can pack for *any* journey is the right state of mind. With that platitude out of the way, the second most important thing to acknowledge is that you will pack more than you will actually need.

This is human nature. While I admire fellow travellers who can go months with a daypack containing just two shirts, two pairs of underwear and a lot of interesting bacteria, I can guarantee they are not travelling with young kids.

Kids can chew up that daypack in a single morning, and still need a new change of clothes by lunch. They do not do laundry, or buy clothes or pack suitcases. That is your responsibility, just as it is to feed them when they are hungry, warm them when they are cold and entertain them when they are bored – at least, until they become teenagers, at which point, they'd rather you didn't have anything to do with them, except give them money.

Every family will need to pack:

➤ Whatever you think you *might* need

➤ Whatever you *might probably* need

➤ Whatever you *might probably* need *at a pinch*

➤ Whatever you probably forgot

The more you pack, the more you will be unpacking, cleaning, carrying and packing again.

The less you pack, the more you will be washing, spot cleaning and thinking of creative ways to entertain kids with books and toys they've long lost interest in.

• •

PACKING TIPS TO KEEP IN MIND

You do not need to travel with a pharmacy

If you need something, buy it along the way, unless you're going to the middle of nowhere, in which case, snake antivenin can be difficult to come by. Toiletries take up a lot more space and weight than people expect.

You do not need to travel with a toyshop

If you need something, buy it along the way. Australia is blessed with a variety of discount stores where toys, books and stationery are staggeringly cheap. Bring toys that inspire imagination games – figurines, bubbles, dolls, colouring books, cards – and that are easy to pack.

You do not need to travel with your entire wardrobe

You need enough clothing for a day in which *anything* can happen, from being invited to a royal event to tramping in the bush.

Since royal invites are probably not forthcoming, one decent dress or shirt will suffice, plus enough shirts, underwear and socks to see you through a week without doing the washing (unless you love doing laundry – to each their own).

Double or triple that rule for clothing options for kids, who have a tendency to burn through clothing like Nero burned through Rome.

Fortunately, kids' clothing does not take up much space.

You do not need to pack a grocery store

Snacks that are nutritious and healthy can be replenished every time you visit a grocery store or petrol station, which you will be doing often. Watch the kids' sugar and lolly intake. Keep snacks in a snack bag or compartment that is easily accessible, and always carry water bottles.

You will start rusty, but gradually become a well-oiled machine

Reading blogs and books might give you an edge, but nobody sets off on a big adventure with their packing dialled in. Within a week, you'll be cursing that you brought X and your last-minute decision to leave Y. Correction: if you have a partner, you'll be cursing *their* decision to bring X and *their* last-minute decision to leave Y.

PRAMS

As soon as she could walk, Raquel always felt more comfortable out of a pram. Her brother, Gali, felt differently about life on wheels, and so on arriving we cast our net for the lightest, easiest single travel pram we could find.

Melbourne-based company Valcobaby's Snap 4 was the perfect pram for our adventure, and off we set, but it turned out we couldn't walk four metres without Raquel wanting to jump into the single pram. In one of the better decisions of our journey, I drove to Valcobaby's office and literally begged for their Snap 4 double, which also happened to be the lightest and

best *double* pram we could find.

Finally, each kid had a side, there was peace in the valley, and we took the Snap 4 everywhere: on treetop walks, to cliff tops, mountains and beaches. Each seat could recline to full sleep mode, not that our kids ever felt inclined to use that feature. Unfortunately, the pram was too small for the adults to use (attempts were made).

Point is: get a good, robust and light pram, and a double if you have two small kids. If you have more than two, nothing I can recommend will save you. Look for a pram that has wheels that rotate smoothly, a simple fold-up and release mechanism, good shade coverage and a bottom pouch to carry things. Most importantly, the pram should be light enough to carry with one hand or have a shoulder strap.

Very young kids will also benefit from a baby carrier or baby backpack. We brought our Ergobaby carrier and used it twice, because once we'd schlepped it halfway around the world, Galileo decided he wanted nothing to do with it. If you have space to bring a baby carrier or backpack, it will save you time and effort, and your shoulder and neck muscles will grow impressively.

Flying with prams

Should you check the pram in with your luggage, or check it at the gate? We found both options were hit and miss.

Depending on the size of the airport, waiting for the pram to show up at the oversized luggage counter added a half-hour to transit, or else the pram magically appeared as we dis-embarked the plane.

Neither of our kids felt partic-ularly excited to stay in the pram at the airport, and nap times were screwed up anyway. Due to its size, we had to check in our double pram regardless.

Travel cots

Another fine decision was investing in an easy-to-set-up travel cot, which was also light to transport. Valcobaby again to the rescue! Yes, they helped us out as sponsors, but only because we begged and pleaded them to.

Their Zephyr Porta Crib is a

cinch to set up and take down for late-night arrivals and rushed morning pack-ups, and most importantly, Galileo really took to it. He loved his little bed, where he would bury his head under a pillow or push up against the netting to get comfortable. We parked it in passageways and wardrobes, in bedrooms and living rooms.

While we battled with Raquel at bedtime, Gali was reliably eager to hit the zeds, and embraced his own consistent environment each night as we dealt with ever-changing mattresses, pillows and room configurations. If only there were travel cribs for adults.

Nappy bags

When it comes to nappies, my wife and I hold different opinions (and elsewhere too, but that's what makes marriage so interesting).

I believe a nappy bag is just a bag that contains nappies, and therefore, the bag can and should resemble any other bag that is practical, comfortable and suits the purpose.

Ana believes a nappy bag should look like a nappy bag, with nooks and crannies for nappies, wipes, change pads, sippy cups, bottles and all the other mysterious stuff mums keep in nappy bags, and their handbags in general.

Certainly, a nappy bag raises fewer red flags from overly diligent airline staff, unless you're flying budget, in which case it will be weighed like every other carry-on bag.

Whatever you go with, make sure everything is accessible, so you don't end up emptying the bag onto the toilet floor in a Hungry Jacks to find the nappy rash cream.

LUGGAGE

I'm a personal fan of the wheeled duffel, which is practical and allows me to jam stuff in without worrying about the rigidity of hard-shell cases.

The only exception is when I'm jamming in something breakable, in which case, an expandable hard shell is the way to go.

If you're driving, luggage must obviously fit in your car/trailer/motorhome. If you're flying, it has to meet airlines' weight restrictions. We were doing both, a lot, and so travelled with a combination of Swiss Gear wheeled duffels and hard shells.

For our family of four, we carried:

- ➤ One medium case/duffel per adult
- ➤ One carry-on case for both kids (with one side for each child's things)
- ➤ One daypack for each adult
- ➤ One daypack for each kid
- ➤ One nappy/snack bag

Eight pieces of luggage total. With the kids running around like hyperactive gibbons, my wife would focus on them and leave loading and transporting luggage to me.

With an overpriced airport trolley, it's all manageable, until you add:

- ➤ One double stroller, empty, because why would the kids want to be in a stroller when they can swing between security barriers?
- ➤ Two bulky car seats
- ➤ One portable crib

Since all of this must be checked in and collected at every airport, it gets interesting. Add to the mix a kid around your shorts, lack of sleep and the stress of rushing because it took an extra thirty minutes to get a maxi cab (an hour if in Adelaide).

There's also hauling all this stuff out of your hotel, into the cab, out of the cab, onto a trolley, into departures, onto the scale and onto the bag-

gage belt . . . and you can understand why so many people looked at this book, had a good laugh, and then picked up a magazine about the secret life of garden gnomes.

During the course of our year-long travels across six countries, we accumulated so much crap that we ended up buying *another* hard-shell case, which filled up with toys, books, towels, clothes too small for one kid but too big for the other, kitchen essentials we got sick of replacing, seasonal clothing for a season we were not in, souvenirs, and all the other burrs that cling to travellers as we make our way through the grasslands of tourism.

Do not leave home *with* an extra suitcase, because the temptation to fill it up at the start will be immense. Just anticipate that you might need one down the line, along with a second overpriced airport trolley.

Packing myths

➤ Does rolling clothing save you space? No, but it sure eats up time.

➤ Can Marie Kondo help? Probably, but this is your life, not a Japanese fad.

➤ Do you need all this stuff? We met families travelling with far less, including one dad who was a committed minimalist. They scaled down to nothing for each flight hop, and then proceeded to replace all that nothing with much the same things as they had before. To each their own.

THE JOY OF TRAILERS

In the driving section of this book (p 182), I sang the praises of a Move Yourself trailer, which was a tremendous help with packing everything into the car. It allowed us to travel with more stuff (particularly food basics), have easy access to essentials and drive in a relatively uncluttered car. With everything else going on, do you need to spend an extra half hour playing Tetris with luggage in your car?

On the downside, parking with a trailer can become a real issue,

especially if you're staying in urban hotels and not caravan parks.

We called ahead to book an extra parking space for our trailer, and I became quite adept at hooking and unhooking it and moving it around to fit in different spaces. My lower back has never forgiven me.

TOYS

When choosing travel toys for your kids, remember: the more pieces, the more picking up. The more expensive, the faster they'll get bored of it.

Other kids' toys are always best, especially if you're staying in another family's Airbnb. Toys that require imagination are great, and toys that contain alarming levels of BPA, formaldehyde and arsenic are not.

You'll be visiting a lot of gift shops, so prepare to be inundated with 'Let's buy this!' and 'Let's buy that!' – first from your partner, then from your kids. Be firm: if you bought a toy at each stop you'd run out of space and money very quickly.

Remember you don't have to bring enough toys to get you through the entire trip. There are bargains to be found at the Reject Shop, dollar stores and department stores. A $5 toy can buy you a few days of peace, after which, don't feel bad leaving stuff behind or donating it to other families on the road.

We often found beach hotels had a trove of abandoned beach toys, so ask the front desk or the pool attendants before buying more spades and buckets to add to their collection.

Pick a Berry

On long trips with younger children, it's important to bring a favourite stuffed toy to give your children emotional support and a sense of stability.

Before we left Canada, we bought Raquel an IKEA panda, which she named Berry, but pronounced 'Bearie' (she insists I make this absolutely clear). My son couldn't give two shits about his stuffed toys, although on a few occasions, he did in fact shit *on* them. Nevertheless, Gali picked up a few gift-shop creatures on the way as cot buddies.

Raquel was never fanatical about her stuffed toys back home, but it quickly became clear that Berry enjoyed a special relationship. Having just flown across the country to Hobart, guess who we managed to forget in our holiday cabin back in Perth?

Raquel was inconsolable, and I knew things were serious when I took her to a toyshop to get a new stuffed toy and she refused to choose one. This is how I came to pay $30 for a stuffed toy to be flown from the Discovery Parks in Perth to the Discovery Parks in Devonport, and how I came to love Discovery Parks in Perth for understanding this was a vital matter of emotional urgency.

A week later, Berry was back in Raquel's loving arms, and indeed, six countries and a year later, she continues to cuddle up to him every night. Had I known the special significance this panda stuffed toy would play in her life, I would have bought something more Australian – a wombat perhaps – and something that wasn't mass-produced for IKEA.

That being said, if we ever lose Berry again, I know exactly where and how to replace him. Point is: if your kids are young enough to feel this level of attachment to a stuffed toy, choose one for them and look after it as if it is a family member.

If you want to be really clever, buy two identical toys and keep one with friends as a back-up, *just in case* you do lose the other on the road, and don't have Discovery Parks to save the day.

Leave the (physical) books

If you've never used an e-reader before, now is the time to invest in one. The space and weight savings are phenomenal.

Alternatively, look for light, second-hand paperback kids' books you can donate or trade as you go.

Flying light

If you're flying with budget airlines as we did, be aware they often weigh carry-on luggage with unnerving diligence, thanks to profit margins. I was out $50 for an extra 1.5 kilograms in my daypack, which contained a laptop, camera, tablet, e-reader, headphones, travel documents and not much else.

You might need to spread some of that weight to the kids' carry-on bags, if only for the weigh-in before boarding.

A kids' backpack you can carry

When it comes to your kids' daypacks, you will be tempted to buy something small and cute with dancing unicorns and decals of animated puppies.

In all likelihood, you'll end up carrying this bag, because small children and infants seldom feel the need to. In which case, small, cute and unicorn-y don't make any practical sense whatsoever.

Find as large a bag as your kid can handle, and make sure you can shoulder it comfortably when he/she tires of it (usually after about five minutes).

Don't forget the last-minute sweep

Despite our best efforts, living in a constant state of flux ensured we initially lost stuff – phone chargers, camera chargers, toys, books – with alarming frequency.

Before long, we made a point of taking the time to do a last-minute sweep before leaving a destination. We checked under the bed, under the couch, in the wall sockets, in the bathroom, in the fridge and in drawers we thought we didn't use but absentmindedly did.

Once this policy was implemented, we hardly lost anything, and were shocked to see how many toys ended up under the hotel couch.

WESTERN

AUSTRALIA

MARGARET RIVER

Make nice with the stingray

 Age minimum: None

 Open: Year round

 Visit: www.margaretriver.com/members/hamelin-bay-beach

With beach and cave adventures for the kids, and booze for the adults, Margaret River is a trifecta bonanza for family holidays. Like us, you might find yourself driving down from Perth, in which case stop by Busselton Jetty, which stretches so far into the sea you need a jetty train to reach the underwater observatory at the other end.

Continuing south, we took another detour for a short hike to the Injidup Natural Spa, where crashing waves wash into a series of rock pools. The thundering waves proved a little too much for our five year old, who was quite happy to watch other kids get harmlessly flushed in the pools.

Eagle Bay Brewing Co proved a stellar choice for lunch, and a tasty insight into why upstart craft breweries are giving the region's famous wineries a run for their merlot. Instead of pretentious tasting rooms, local breweries draw punters with great food, playgrounds and, in this case, a huge shaded sandpit full of toys. Happy kids make happy parents, and a crisp IPA after a long drive makes a happy parent happier still.

Surfing is a major drawcard in Margaret River, although the

famously big swells go well over
the heads of younger children.
Fortunately for those whose children

aren't quite up to hitting the waves,
there's plenty of action on shore.
About a half-hour's drive from
Margaret River is beautiful Hamelin
Bay. What distinguishes this bay's
white sands and turquoise waters
from the region's other white sandy
beaches with turquoise waters are the
stingrays that frequently patrol the
shoreline, searching for scraps from
fishermen.

So reliable is the food source
that the rays wash up right on the
beach, allowing you to literally
hand-feed them as they do. Smooth
rays are the dark-coloured giants,
while the smaller, wing-tipped
eagle rays are just as curious.

During our visit, a friendly

local was handing out baitfish for the kids. Despite what might be suggested by the high-profile tragedy of Steve Irwin, whose death was attributed to a smooth ray, the rays here are docile and there have been no reported incidents.

This unique marine wildlife encounter is harmless for all concerned, although definitely watch where you put your feet. It's also worthwhile reinforcing to kids the idea that animals are unpredictable. The size of the rays will do the rest to deter kids from getting out of hand.

Nervous at first, my daughter gradually got closer to the beaching rays until she gently touched one and squealed with delight. Stingrays have excellent hearing, but unlike me and my quivering eardrums, this one didn't seem bothered at all.

Your best bet to encounter the rays in Hamelin Bay is to visit between 9am and 10am, or when the fishing boats return in the early afternoon with their welcome scraps. If you're not in a rush, it's a wonderful beach to chill on for the day, and is part of a protected marine reserve with camping and a caravan park nearby. In a region chock full of highlights, feeding rays in Hamelin Bay proved to be ours.

PRINCIPALITY OF HUTT RIVER

Not your average prince

 Age minimum: None

 Open: Year round

 Visit: www.principality-hutt-river.com

My daughter's eyes turned into saucers when I told her we were off to meet the Prince of Hutt River. Just imagine . . . a real-life prince!

We've strived to insulate Raquel from the glossy Disney canon of films and stories with distraught maidens in desperate need of a charming prince. We prefer a version of Cinderella in which she kickboxes her abusive stepmother and confidently makes her own way into the world, no knight in shining armour necessary. Still . . . a real-life prince!

Driving north from Geraldton along National Route 1, we turned left onto a dirt road in dry, rolling farmland. Our destination was the Principality of Hutt River, a contentious micronation that seceded from Australia in 1970.

Raquel was expecting something akin to Neuschwanstein Castle in the Bavarian Alps, the castle that has inspired fairytale palaces from Snow White to Shrek. The Hutt River reality was a dusty road that led to a modest red-brick building with signs reading 'Government Offices' and 'Post Office'.

Inside was Prince Graeme, an affable chap who succeeded his dad Prince Leonard as Head of State. We learned all about the fascinating and somewhat bizarre story of Hutt River, which is more the tale of a

family's fight for land rights than one of hubris or eccentricity.

As Prince Graeme stamped our

passports with a visa, he explained how his family initially battled a controversial wheat board, has appealed to international trade organisations and even invoked the Geneva Convention. In a humble nearby building is the Principality Museum, where Prince Leonard showed us cases of diplomatic paraphernalia while rapid-firing stories about his legal triumphs and injustices.

The Principality has more than 13,000 honorary citizens around the world, its own mint and international diplomats. It all goes a bit over the heads of the kids, who gravitated towards a giant clay sculpture outside of Prince

Leonard's winking head, flanked by two robot-looking statues made of assorted junk.

There's a campground in Nain, the self-proclaimed capital where all the buildings sit, including a chapel honouring the late Princess Shirley, Graeme's mum. We stayed for several hours, bought some snacks and one of our more memorable souvenir T-shirts.

Continuing on our journey towards Shark Bay, we debated the genius and/or folly of Australia's most famous micronation; for there are others, including the Grand Duchy of Avram in Tasmania, an empire in New South Wales and a kingdom in Queensland. The Principality of Hutt River is the oldest and most respected of the bunch, having formal relations with Taiwan and a letter of acknowledgment from the Queen of England herself (on display in the museum).

As for the kids, they got to meet a prince, pick up a rather unique stamp in their passport, and, perhaps more importantly, learn about the large gap between fantasy and reality.

WA MARITIME MUSEUM

Is that megamouth?

 Age minimum: None, but kids aged up to fifteen enter free

 Open: Year round, closed Good Friday, Christmas Day, Boxing Day, New Year's Day

 Visit: www.museum.wa.gov.au/museums/maritime

For kids, museums can often feel like an informational desert island without a single coconut tree of joy. Great family-friendly museums supplement information with larger-than-life displays, interactive exhibits, big images, music, dress-up and, most importantly, staff who enjoy engaging with kids.

The WA Maritime Museum is one such place, where young and old landlubbers alike celebrate the unique relationship between humans and sea. Located on the coast of historic Fremantle, the WA Maritime Museum has several galleries with plenty of illuminated space to run about and explore.

We arrived in time for a free highlights tour at 10:30am, which introduced the kids to huge exhibits that ranged from the victorious *America II* racing yacht to the *Parry Endeavour* that Jon Sanders used to circumnavigate the world three times solo.

Outside is the Oberon-class submarine HMAS *Ovens*, a cold war–era vessel. To see and actually board these different kinds of vessels was fascinating, especially since my family takes to sailing

the way vegans take to butcheries – funny tummy, anyone?

In the WA Down Under Gallery, the kids learned about the region's marine life. They made shadows in a small room projecting

underwater footage, and were spellbound by the remains of a rare prehistoric-looking shark called the megamouth. Only fifty specimens have ever been found of this bottom-dweller filter feeder, blessed with a shy nature and a great name.

There are a lot of exhibits and a lot of reading, so the kids naturally steered towards the craft tables set up during the school holidays. Friendly staff helped them cut, paste and draw, while an interactive device that let them colour boats on a screen kept them rapt.

This destination earns bonus points for the dress-up area, where the kids could don the garb of pirates, sailors and Romans (in line with a visiting exhibit about

Pompeii). For the younger kids, there's a play area with books, games and toys upstairs, and of course, a coffee shop to keep the wind in parents' sails.

When I arrived, late because of an appointment, I let my daughter guide me to her favourite exhibits, listening to her as she excitedly shared what she'd learned. She didn't always get the facts right, but her enthusiasm was faultless.

We skipped the Shipwrecks Gallery because the sordid tale of the *Batavia* – including skeletal remains of victims of this notorious shipwreck – along with other wrecks might have tainted our newly discovered appreciation of maritime triumphs and wonder.

As museums go, the WA Maritime Museum was anything but dry, but then, we should have guessed that from its very name. Note that my editor thinks that particular line deserves applause for being "the daddest of dad jokes." Thank you. As for this experience, it's what we're talking about when we say travel is the best education for kids, and why a good museum is better than any classroom.

CAVERSHAM
WILDLIFE PARK

Pleasing the mob

 Age minimum: None. Kids younger than three years old enter free

 Open: Year round, closed Christmas Day

 Visit: www.cavershamwildlife.com.au

After long days in the car driving up and down the Western Australian coast, the kids were becoming a little cranky. Time to pull out a trump card – and I don't mean building a pointless wall between the rear and front of the car.

Instead, bring the smiles back with a stop at the largest privately owned collection of native wildlife in the state. About a half-hour's drive north-east of Perth's city centre, it was far enough for Galileo to fall asleep on the way, and for Raquel to somehow use her foot to mess with the air conditioning so that hot air was pumping into the back, directly onto her sweating brother's face.

We couldn't – and still can't – take our eyes off that girl for a second, unless she was in an enclosure with kangaroos and wallabies, and endless pellets to feed them. It had only been a few weeks since Raquel's first encounter with roos, when she chased a wild mob all over a golf course in the Dandenongs in Victoria. I remember that day clearly because she got a little too close to a fierce-looking boomer – a parenting fail, I know, but what

does a Canadian know about kangaroos?

Having pellets spoon-fed to them all day made this Caversham mob a lot more welcoming, and Raquel would have happily fed the

jills and joeys all afternoon. But there's a lot to do at the park and the promise of touching a wombat was all the enticement needed.

The park's free shows are staggered throughout the day, making a morning or afternoon visit equally convenient. Meet Wombat and Friends was our first stop. We were ushered into a barn where we could do a circuit to meet handlers and their various animals. We got to pose with a fuzzy, overgrown pompom better known as a southern hairy-nosed wombat, touch a woma python, gently brush a woylie, meet a northern blue-tongued lizard and chat to a rather chirpy gang-gang cockatoo.

Next up were the koalas,

penguins and petting zoo. Our two year old was a little more cautious around the creatures and critters, although seemed to enjoy the signs a lot, pointing them out with an 'E-I-E-I-O' at every opportunity. He was at that age where new words were sprouting every day – words like 'apple' and 'ig!' and also 'where the hell are you taking me? I'm only eighteen months old!'

Okay, maybe not the last one, but his look said it all. Caversham has the usual Aussie wildlife suspects: dingoes, Tassie devils, echidnas, emus and more in various enclosures along the leafy, shaded pathways that encircle the kangaroo enclosure.

The goal of any reputable wildlife park is to educate its visitors about conservation and raise awareness for the animals native to Australia, eighty per cent of which are unique to the country.

Fun and manageable for toddlers and tots, Caversham is easily one of the premier parks in the country, and a great place to stretch your legs if you're travelling through Perth.

ROTTNEST ISLAND

Just don't touch the quokka

 Age minimum: None

 Open: Year round

 Visit: www.rottnestexpress.com.au

'We've seen your video of Rottnest Island pop up on Facebook, but we were shocked to see the children touching the quokkas. We encourage a reasonable distance between humans and wildlife. This includes not touching the quokka.'

I received this email from the marketing folks at Rottnest Island, shortly after I posted a video of our family day trip there. I mention this because, firstly, getting a selfie with a quokka on the island has become *the* thing to do, with the same marketing folks relishing thousands of inadvertently promotional selfies and videos. Tennis star Roger Federer's quokka selfie was reposted more than half a million times, go Rotto!

Unfortunately, getting the requisite selfie probably involves violating whatever reasonable distance you should keep between face and quokka, although these curious marsupials don't seem the least bit bothered. Their lack of predators, jolly nature and goofy expressions made the #quokkaselfie a thing in the first place.

Secondly, putting toddlers in close proximity to a small marsupial

– which resembles the cute stuffed toys sold in gift shops – without the kids instinctively reaching out to touch one can prove a challenge. *Especially* when you're trying to make a video and get a selfie at the same time.

'Please guys, *don't* touch the quokka. I said, don't touch the quokka! Okay, if you touch that quokka, it will bite you with massive venomous fangs, because that's what Australian animals do!'

That last one worked, but in order to prevent a lifelong phobia of marsupials, I quickly told them I was confusing quokka with vipers. Point of all this is: do your best to prevent the kids from touching the quokka.

Rottnest Island sits about a half-hour ferry-ride offshore from Perth. It's a protected nature reserve with a long naval and convict history, and is famous for pristine bays, beaches and the aforementioned quokka.

Rottnest receives about 600,000 visitors a year, and it's all foot traffic. You can rent bikes and explore by pedal, or train or coach around the island. No motorised vehicles can be brought onto the island without permission.

We woke up early to catch the Rottnest Express departing from Fremantle. It's a notoriously rough crossing, but our fast ferry crashed through the waves, and ginger drops helped immensely.

Once on the island, we picked up our rental bikes with a back seat for Raquel and a pull-carriage for Galileo. We rode around the dusty streets of the main settlement, past old prison colony accommodation that's now rented out as self-catering cabins.

Then we hopped on a train to visit the massive artillery gun and spooky tunnels at Oliver Hill. The conductor let Raquel ride up front and blow the whistle, which made it her best. day. ever. That is, until she met the quokkas!

Trains, it has to be said, will always take a back seat to approachable, oversized squirrels. On a coach tour around the island, we visited gorgeous bays where we spotted osprey nests, dolphins and tired tourists riding bicycles in the baking January heat. The kids were exhausted but held up pretty well.

Rewarded with ice-cream back at the settlement in Thompson Bay, we caught the 4:25pm ferry home. The swells were huge, but Raquel loved the crashing waves, giving each swell a name. Gali fell asleep and my wife desperately needed more ginger drops.

We returned to Perth exhausted, wishing we could have spent three to four days exploring the island at our own pace, overnighting at one of the wide selection of accommodation options. Still, our big Rotto day trip was well worth it, even if it did piss off a few marketing people.

KINGS PARK

A big park to get lost in

 Age minimum: None

 Open: Year round

 Visit: www.bgpa.wa.gov.au/kings-park

According to a Western Australian government website, ninety-eight per cent of all foreign and domestic tourists to Perth will find themselves in Kings Park and Botanic Garden. Bigger than Hyde Park in London and Central Park in New York, Kings Park is home to 3000 species of native Western Australian fauna, seventy bird species, historic war memorials, important statues and plenty of attractions to keep the kids busy.

As we drove into the park under a rich blue sky framed by bare trunks of lemon-scented gums, the manicured gardens of the Fraser Street entrance contrasted with the wild scrub and bush that made up two-thirds of the park. We headed straight for the surreal-looking thirty-six ton Gija Jumulu boab tree, an iconic landmark that was trucked in from the Kimberley region to save it from roadworks.

It's a fitting entrance to the Botanic Garden, where thousands of native plants are meticulously arranged in different sections. From here, the kids bolted for the Lotterywest Federation Walkway, a 620-metre-long path that includes a striking arched bridge high among the treetops. It offers fifty-two metres of glass and steel embedded in nature, with stellar views of the city and coastline, and

is the kind of attraction most cities would charge for.

But the real fun for kids lies at Rio Tinto Naturescape, an ambitious playground designed to connect kids to the surrounding landscape. Spanning six hectares, Naturescape features two aerial walkways, a wading creek and watering hole, climbing ropes, tunnels and a special area to build a cubby.

Another play area, the May Drive Parkland, offers a mist forest, life-size dinosaur replicas to scramble all over, and many other playground favourites. On the park's northern boundary is the Ivey Watson Playground, specifically designed for kids under six. You'll find planes, pirate ships, slides and plenty of shade too.

Off Saw Avenue is another nature-based play area, Variety Place, which has a fort, climbing net, bridges and climbing logs. If all of this is just what's on offer for kids, you can understand why so many people visit Kings Park. Highlights for adults include the art gallery, summer performances, Jacob's Ladder stair climb, Moonlight Cinema, walking trails and Australia's largest annual flower exhibition.

With views of the Swan River, CDB skyscrapers and the Darling Mountains, Kings Park is an ideal spot to get your Perth bearings and enjoy a fresh gum-scented breeze to the soundtrack of kids playing their hearts out.

OCEAN PARK AQUARIUM,
SHELL BEACH AND HAMELIN POOL

Nature in action

 Age minimum: None

 Open: Year round, closed Christmas Day and Boxing Day

 Visit: www.oceanpark.com.au/aquarium-tours

Australia's beautiful beaches were once all rocks and shells, which slowly eroded over millennia into the soft sandy stuff we know and love. Pulling off the highway into the Shark Bay World Heritage Area, we discovered a beach that still needs a few thousand years to join the club.

Countless tiny Shark Bay cockle-shells fill up the aptly named Shell Beach, a sixty-kilometre stretch of coastline with shells up to ten metres deep. Eventually this will all become sand, but for now it's a perfect example of the sweeping and unusual natural phenomena that make this region so famous.

We had spent the previous night in the shipping container–like box that's been converted into the family room in the Hamelin Pool Caravan Park. Some hilarious local characters operated the humble park, and the stars that night spar-kled so hard it almost punished our eyes to look at them.

Hamelin Pool is home to a geological marvel: the world's largest 'living' network of fossils, called stromatolites, which slowly

grow over millennia. Stromatolites have been around for a whopping eighty per cent of Earth's 4.5-billion-year history, making them the oldest macrofossils in existence. While Hamelin Pool's examples might be a staggering 3.7 billion years old, they look just like ocean rocks.

It's difficult to grasp the concept of eons of evolution when you're five, and having driven in a straight line for several days, the kids demanded action. Fortunately, the Ocean Park Aquarium came to the rescue. Located just south of Denham and thirty-three kilometres from Monkey Mia, this unassuming facility is ideal for curious young kids.

Marine biologists perform hourly tours, allowing you to join the circuit at any point, and meet some of the marine creatures that call the western tip of Western Australia home.

With wide eyes, the kids peered into various tanks holding sea snakes, venomous rockfish, stingrays, turtles, puffer fish, moon wrasse and other fish. We finally learned the difference between venomous and poisonous (a mistake most adults get wrong): you *eat* poison; you get *bitten* with venom . . . So stop telling me about your poisonous snakes, because I have no plans to eat one!

We also learned that Shark Bay got its name from European sailors who saw countless nervous sharks swimming in the bay. Nervous sharks are an actual species, known for their shyness around people.

Although these particular ones are harmless, sharks always make people nervous, so the name is kind of perfect. The aquarium tour includes a visit to the onsite Shark Lagoon to watch the lemon shark feeding, the kind of activity that feels entirely apt in a place called Shark Bay.

All the tanks and exhibits seem to pay particular attention to meeting little kids' eye level, and there are opportunities to touch and feel too. I'm awarding bonus points for the onsite restaurant that serves meals of a quality we didn't expect in a roadside attraction. Shell Beach and Ocean Park were fantastic introductions to the region as we continued onward to Denham.

MONKEY MIA

The last sunset in Australia

 Age minimum: None

 Open: Year round

 Visit: www.monkeymiawildsights.com.au

We missed waking up early enough to catch the first sunrise in Australia, a fiery yolk popping over the horizon in Cape Byron, New South Wales.

On the opposite coast, it's easier and far more fun to enjoy the last Australian sunset on a sailboat off Monkey Mia. Located about twenty-five kilometres from Denham in the Shark Bay World Heritage Area, Monkey Mia is a popular marine park famous for the bottlenose dolphins that visit the beach up to three times a day to be fed.

It all started innocently enough: local fishermen would feed curious dolphins, which quickly made a habit of swimming up to the beach. As word got out, the number of tourists wanting to participate in the activity proved detrimental to the dolphins, impacting their natural rhythms and birth rates.

Today, onsite park rangers strictly control the encounter, with

ten per cent of the dolphins' feed carefully distributed among the visiting pod. Having read all about Monkey Mia, I excitedly told the kids they'd have the chance to hand-feed a real-life dolphin, which was a mistake.

Just four people were selected from dozens of tourists on the beach, crushing many a kid's (and adult's) dream of a special wildlife encounter. Small fish were dropped into the mouth of a dolphin, and within seconds the whole thing was over, with more than one tourist moping off wondering if *this* was the reason they just drove nine hours from Perth.

My advice: don't tell your kids anything about feeding dolphins and let them simply enjoy the chance to see these beautiful ocean mammals up close on the beach. Too many expectations can sink too many wondrous experiences. We had far better luck walking along the adjacent jetty to the sixty-foot sailing catamaran, the Wildsights Cruises *Shotover*.

Shark Bay has the planet's largest and richest area of seagrass meadows, which are home to the one of the largest dugong populations in the world and a healthy number of sharks, turtles, whales, rays and dolphins. Seeing any or all of these creatures while sailing the turquoise seas would be a joy, even

more so because the bay is so calm there's an actual guarantee you won't get seasick.

What's more, Wildsights has an 'animal warranty', under which, if you don't see enough wildlife, you can return on any cruise as often as you like until you do. There's even a money-back satisfaction guarantee, which is an impressive case of putting money where your dugong's mouth is.

Our three-hour-long morning cruise departed conveniently shortly after the second dolphin feed at 10am. It didn't take long before we spotted our first pair of dugongs, their tails and tips resembling a cross between a dolphin and a whale.

The *Shotover* dropped anchor and we had an opportunity to swim and snorkel, a particular thrill in a place called Shark Bay. Don't worry, people have been swimming out here for a long time, and the last attack was decades ago.

The kids made fast friends with other kids on the boat, bouncing on the net up front and humoured by the friendly Captain Toby. We returned later that afternoon for the ninety-minute sunset sail on the *Shotover,* feeling warm wind in our hair and listening to the sound of movement without motors. We all had a turn to take the captain's wheel, and while we didn't spot any wildlife, it was easily the most magical sunset of our entire journey.

VALLEY OF THE GIANTS

High on eucalypts

 Age minimum: None, kids younger than six years old enter free

 Open: Year round,close Christmas Day

 Visit: www.valleyofthegiants.com.au

This is a book full of things to do with kids, but here's one thing you *shouldn't* do: climb the Dave Evans Bicentennial Tree. At seventy-five-metres high, the world's tallest tree climb is no place for toddlers and tots, young adults or anyone of sound mind and body.

It's featured in this book because it's absolutely worth stopping by on your drive from Margaret River to Albany. Standing at the foot of the trunk, you may be tempted to think, 'Hey, my kids are good climbers, this will be fun'.

That thought will last exactly as long as it takes you to scale to the fourth metal spike jammed into this towering karri giant, which is

a highlight of the forests of Warren National Park.

At that point, you'll notice: your partner getting very agitated, the wide gaps between the spikes as they spiral up the tree, and your kids either crying to get down or screaming with joy to continue upward.

There are no waivers to sign, no reassuring safety nets, and no adults around to advise you *this is not a good idea*. That's why I'm here, telling you this is not a good idea. A good idea would be to stop and admire this impressive fire lookout tree, and then drive onward through various national parks and state forests until you reach the Valley of the Giants Tree Top Walk.

Yes, that's much better parenting, well done. You will have found yourself in the Walpole Wilderness Area, which spans seven national parks along with various nature reserves and conservation zones. To get among the forests of giant tingle, karri and jarrah – species that make up some of the world's tallest trees – you enter through the Valley of the Giants gift shop and stroll along the wooden boardwalk to the 600-metre-long suspended Tree Top Walkway.

As you walk forty metres above the forest floor, rest assured this steel structure all but traps your kids with safety. Gaze out at forests of giant eucalypts that are found nowhere else in the world – including the rest of Australia – and rest easy knowing you don't have to climb any of them.

The elevated walkway even accommodated our double stroller. Once you get to the bottom, there

are easy boardwalk trails where you can breathe in the earthy forest air and keep an eye out for wildlife.

We spotted a wayward quokka, which must have got lost somewhere on the way to Rottnest Island (and was in no mood for a selfie). Due to the size of the wilderness area, nothing here is particularly close, but if you have another hour's drive in you, or are spending the night in Denmark, it's worth checking out the Mount Frankland

Wilderness Lookout, a 600-metre return walk with a 360-degree view of the western portion of the area.

Older kids might want to join you on the slightly longer and steeper hike to the summit. The forests in this region are spectacular and, depending on whether you heed my advice on the Bicentennial Tree (and how the kids behave in the car) you don't even have to risk life and limb to enjoy them.

THE JEWEL CAVE

Who's afraid of the dark?

 Age minimum: Recommended for kids four years and older, kids younger than four enter free

 Open: Year round, closed Christmas Day

 Visit: www.margaretriver.com/jewel-cave-augusta

The caves we visited in Naracoorte, South Australia, were a good warm-up for the largest and most spectacular show cave in Western Australia, the Jewel Cave.

Formed over hundreds of thousands of years, it is part of a large limestone ridge – the result of sand, shells and coral blown in from the coast. Before its discovery, these same winds would blow out of a hole in the ground that locals called, you guessed it, the Wind Hole.

Eventually some brave lads lowered themselves into the hole in the late 1950s and discovered a massive chamber, two kilometres of passage, and some extraordinary rock formations. They also found bones of various animals, including a 400- to 500-year-old possum skeleton and the remains of a

Tasmanian tiger, a carnivore that clearly roamed a little further from Hobart than people at the time realised.

As we entered via the interpretive centre, my daughter was eager to join the hour-long tour to see stalactites and stalagmites, which she could now correctly distinguish. (Remember, stalagmites have a 'g', and therefore grow from the ground, unlike stalactites with a 'c', which start at the ceiling.)

We decided it best to leave our toddler out of this one, because we'd have to descend and ascend two hundred steps into the cave forty-two metres below. Galileo would likely insist either on climbing the stairs by himself (a disaster waiting to happen) or on me carrying him the entire way (also a disaster waiting to happen).

The cave's entrance chamber is massive, and the rock formations did not disappoint. Our enthusiastic guide was quite at home in the caves, and also chattering with the inquisitive kids on the tour.

He pointed out one of the longest straw stalactites found anywhere in the country, the neuron-like helictites, the pendulites and flowstone. Raquel was particularly enamoured with cave coral, which look like the baleen of whales.

Caves might be dark but they definitely light up the imagination. Formations here have nicknames like the Frozen Waterfall and the Organ Pipes. When Raquel's attention began to wander to the dark recesses of the cave, I dispelled her thoughts of monsters by asking her to name various other formations lit by spotlights, a game she excelled at. Another Masterclass in Distraction.

We continued in single file on a narrow metal walkway until we reached the obligatory part of any cave tour where the guide demonstrates just how black it is when the lights turn off. This is a good time to pick up any younger kids, who will likely close their eyes anyway.

Unless you're Daredevil, in which case, you shouldn't have any issues.

Our short moments in pure, blessed and immaculate darkness did the trick to remind everyone on the tour how lovely it would be to return to daylight, like, soon. Particularly when there's a coffee shop to grab a flat white, and a souvenir store for the kids to bargain unsuccessfully for yet another stuffed toy.

Between Mammoth Cave, Lake Cave, Calgardup Cave and others, there are plenty of subterranean wonders to explore around Margaret River. If you're going to choose one, you may as well make it the jewel of the lot.

THE OLD MARRON FARM

Yabbie Dabbie Do

 Age minimum: None, kids three years old and younger enter free

 Open: Year round, closed on Good Friday, Christmas Eve, Christmas Day, and Boxing Day

 Visit: www.albanymarronfarm.com.au

Is there anyone happier than a toddler on an animal farm? Is there anything sillier-looking than an adult on a segway?

You can answer both these questions at a delightful little spot called The Old Marron Farm, a place we didn't have high hopes for, and which, naturally, turned out to be one of our Western Australian highlights. Owned and operated by a welcoming couple, Sharon and Karl, The Old Marron Farm is exactly that . . . an old marron farm that never quite took off commercially, evolving instead into the kind of roadside attraction young kids dream about. Marron, in case you were wondering, are a type of prized freshwater crayfish.

Located thirty kilometres east of Albany on the way to some

spectacular beaches, the farm is home to various animals for the kids to play with and gawk at: horses, ponies, parrots, guinea pigs, rabbits, chickens, emus, a peacock, donkeys and an especially

large pig named Percy. Remember, put a bunny in the arms of a small child and you'll be crowned #Parentoftheyear.

The farm also features an impressive aviary, with parrots that would happily turn the uncontrollable curly locks of my daughter into a healthy nest. When a staff member volunteered to keep the kids busy for a half-hour, Sharon took my wife and me on an off-road segway tour around the property.

I've had opportunities to segway all around the world and it always surprises me that something this ridiculous can be so enjoyable. Moving while standing, using balance to guide your vehicle back and forth – it takes a few minutes to get the hang of it, but soon enough you're cruising through the trees on a sci-fi–inspired contraption.

If The Old Marron Farm feels like

you're visiting friends with cool toys, it's because you are. The Old Marron Farm is not a petting zoo or a wildlife park, just the passion project of a family that has literally built it all themselves. And of course, let's not forget the marron and the yabbies.

Yabbies are a much smaller type of crayfish, and are regarded as a pest species to the larger, often spectacularly blue-hued marron. Both are served up fresh from the farm's Nippers Café, along with smoked trout, sandwiches, pizza and desserts.

My daughter was initially wary

of the taste plate, which featured a butterflied marron served with yabbies in their shell and seafood dipping sauce. We tucked in, and discovered both to be as tasty as any lobster or prawn.

Bidding farewell to the farm, we continued onward to Two Peoples Bay Nature Reserve, and to the stunning turquoise waters, white sands and granite boulders of Little Beach. At low tide, head left on the trail from the car park and explore the rocks and pools, and listen to waves crashing against the shore. No wonder Karl said this is his favourite place in the country.

Having packed our visit to Western Australia with all sorts of fabulous adventures, a visit to The Old Marron Farm reminded us that a young kid's bucket list will always be much simpler than our own.

NATIONAL ANZAC CENTRE

Lest we forget

 Age minimum: Recommended for kids older than seven years, but kids under five years old enter free

Open: Year round, closed Christmas Day

Visit: www.nationalanzaccentre.com.au

I'd love to tell my kids that life is all sparkly ponies and adventure rainbows, and that history is a bouncy pillow of love and joy. It's a difficult question: at what point do you expose young kids to the brutal reality of war?

As with sex, drugs and rock'n'roll, it's probably best kids learn about touchy subjects from their parents before they jump in with their friends. Australia's meat-grinder history in World War I is not child's play, which is one of the reasons I left the kids back at the hotel when I visited the Australian War Memorial in Canberra.

While my daughter would have enjoyed seeing suspended fighter planes, I'm pretty sure the graphic dioramas, weapons, gas masks and subject matter would have opened a can of worms no Disney princess could put back into place.

I wasn't yet a teenager when I watched a Laurence Olivier–narrated documentary series called *The World at War* on Sunday afternoons with my Dad. I still can't shake memories of what I saw: black-and-white footage depicting carnage, destruction and horror. For this reason, I was hesitant to enter the National Anzac Centre in Albany with my kids, especially since the centre's website does not recommend visiting with children seven years or younger.

Still, it felt like something we had to do, and I'd heard encouraging feedback about the interactive and approachable nature of the exhibits. The centre is located in

Albany because this was the very port where 41,000 Australians left for Europe in two large shipping convoys. Too many of them never made it home.

The centre honours the story of the Anzacs through interactive multimedia displays, housed within a striking building overlooking King George Sound, and surrounded by peaceful, lush parkland. From the parade ground of the Princess Royal Fortress you can stroll up the Convoy Walk to a lookout on the summit of Mount Adelaide, reading interpretative boards along the way.

Kids and guns shouldn't mix, but outside the centre is a naval gun collection where the kids can sit and look down the barrel of World War II-era cannons. One of the guns allowed me to rotate its

positioning using a lever, a little ride the kids thoroughly enjoyed, oblivious to the fact we were riding a death machine designed to blow enemies out of the sky.

Inside the centre itself, the mood is decidedly more sombre. We were handed mobile headsets and a series of cards with personal stories of actual people, following their journey through different aspects of the war.

There's a lot of information to digest here, and the kids will likely gravitate to the bronze statue of a solider feeding his horse, and the large picture window looking out to sea. It wasn't too busy during our visit, so we spent some time exploring the exhibits before the kids got too rowdy for the space.

Whether you think your own kids will give you any time at all will determine if you decide to take them inside or not. One option is to have one parent explore the museum while the other takes the kids to explore the fortress, or for something to nibble on in Garrison, the adjacent family-run restaurant.

Either way, with its sweeping views, big weapons and vital story-telling, no visit to Albany could be complete without driving up to the National Anzac Centre.

THE GAP AND
NATURAL BRIDGE

Mind the Gap

 Age minimum: None, but keep an eye on the kids

 Open: Year round

 Visit: www.parks.dpaw.wa.gov.au/park/torndirrup

Powerful, awesome and destructive forces of nature can best be experienced during an earthquake, cyclone, tornado or storm.

Unfortunately, nothing good comes from experiencing an earthquake, cyclone, tornado or storm. We know this because, beyond topographical destruction, these phenomena could be aptly compared to a four year old's melt-down (when, for example, a banana isn't peeled in the correct manner).

Kids are bowled over by nature's extreme forces because they're a lot more exciting than listening to stories about the millions of years of erosion required to create a natural bridge of granite, or carve a

channel between forty-metre high rock cliffs.

Watching the full might of the Southern Ocean slam into the abovementioned channel, on the other hand, is something you can *feel*, especially if you're standing on a raised viewing platform that lets you absorb the shudder of the crashing waves, and feel the salty spray on your skin.

The Gap is a natural formation in Torndirrup National Park, located about twenty minutes' drive from Albany. From the car park, it's an easy hundred-metre walk along a wide cement pathway that feels particularly exposed to the elements (I'd recommend you save this one for a sunny day).

Although the extended metal viewing platform can withstand

the elements, your nerves might not withstand the open spaces in the flooring that juts out from the granite cliff. Supported by rock anchors embedded nine metres deep, the platform protrudes ten metres over the cliff. I kept thinking of those London Underground announcements urging passengers to 'Mind the gap' – as if this particular gap gives you any other choice.

Howling wind, thunderous waves and ocean spray awed both the adults and the kids. A short walk away is the Natural Bridge, a striking granite archway formed by smashing waves. There are also blowholes, which make a belly-deep *whomp* sound when ocean rushes in beneath,

each *boom!* setting off high-pitched squeals from the children.

Although we visited The Gap during peak summer, we were the only ones there for the late-afternoon sunset, adding to a tingling sense of isolation. In winter, when even fewer people visit the area, you might have company, as whales migrate off the coast.

It's worth noting that the exposed conditions and slippery rocks make this region particularly hairy, so keep your feet to the paths, and your eyes on the kids. Nature's forces are awesome, immense and powerful, best experienced without any potential hazards – and that includes banana peels.

ON THE ROAD

Long drives are a grim reality for any great Australian family journey. Road trips are practical, they're cost-effective and they hover somewhere between transcendent adventure and hell on asphalt.

Every family has its own coping mechanisms to ensure the kids don't turn into road demons during long drives: mind-numbing car games, mind-numbing music, podcasts, don't-judge-me-it-works screens.

Some kids enjoy the car; they settle down, peer out the window at the world in motion and fall to blissful sleep while their parents argue about directions. Other kids would sooner be put in a straightjacket at a lolly store than spend one minute in a car seat. Some kids don't get sick, while others are prone to projectile vomit their Milo cereal right on the back of your neck (here's looking at you Galileo).

Yep, every kid is different, which makes it particularly challenging when you have two *different* kids in the same family.

We drove about 20,000 kilometres across Australia, finessing our road trips into a fine art – and by fine art, I'm referring to the work of Jackson Pollock, since our car interior often resembled his finest work.

Let's examine the facets of the family road trip with a view to finessing your own.

• •

THE CAR

It's quite possible you once had a Dream Machine: two doors, wide treads, loud exhaust, a real head-turner. Upon having children, you likely realised your head-turner could now more accurately be described as a spine-cracker. With kids, any vehicle that quickly and easily packs them in along with all their crap (and avoids giving you a neck, shoulder and back injury in the process) is the *real* dream machine. For a long family road trip, the bigger the vehicle, the better things will be. Don't worry, there's always a mid-life crisis to look forward to, when the kids move out and you can return to a sporty convertible, spraining your vertebrae when you squeeze into the low driver seat. We scaled the highs and lows of Australian family

travel in a comfortable eight-seater Ford Everest. It even turned a few heads. Whatever vehicle you take on your trip, make sure it's mechanically reliable, has air conditioning, the ability to play music on demand and can survive at least one unfortunate marsupial impact.

Car seats

Kids need regulation-compliant car seats; it's the law, and like so many laws, car seats can be complicated and occasionally unnecessary.

Yes, you probably remember sleeping across the whole back seat when

you were a kid, nary a seat belt in sight. I remember sleeping on the floor of the back seat while my older brother got the bench. I had to carefully curl around the rusted hole that inexplicably appeared in the floor of my mum's pale blue 1970 Ford Escort. As with asbestos, cigarettes and playing games that involved stuffing our heads in plastic bags, this approach to travel safety is best left in the past.

Car seats are a serious business these days, complicated by international standards that aren't very international, and hard-moulded plastic that expires. We couldn't bring our Canadian car seats over, because Australian authorities evidently believe that using a Canadian car seat is as risky as kicking a moose bull in the balls. Meanwhile in Canada, anyone caught placing a toddler in an Australian car seat is forced to snort Vegemite. It should be noted that most car seats are manufactured in China, where children aren't required to use them at all.

Procuring a car seat is a rite of passage for every new parent, as is the queasy feeling that somewhere, someone is having a good laugh each time you're forced to decline a perfectly fine second-hand seat because of an arbitrary expiry date.

The kids are safe, though, which is all that matters. Although, they'd also be safe if we made them wear crash helmets and a life vest, just in case they got caught in a particularly nasty hail storm.

After leaving Australia, we travelled across Asia for four months, and our kids were unleashed without car seats in cars, tuktuks, wagons, buses, bikes and scooters.

Having them unrestrained somehow made the trips less of an ordeal, although this was not the case for every Asian road trip – a fair portion of which result in crashes and end rather badly for both the vehicle and the passengers within.

For all our miles travelled, we were spared any incidents, save for being rear-ended at a Melbourne intersection by a texting driver. (Put the damn phone down!) Our high-quality Britax car seats ensured neither kid felt any repercussions, unlike the vehicle's complicated rear camera sensor system.

It's best to err on the side of caution and strap your kids up nice and tight. Also, it's worth remembering that car seats are the next best thing to a straitjacket.

Handy tips

➤ If you're flying and renting cars, invest in seats that are light and don't require an engineering degree to install.

➤ When buckling in your kid, be ready for face punches or kisses, either of which might occur when your face is too close and too vulnerable to the whims of a small child.

➤ Pay careful attention to how you disassemble the cover for cleaning, because you're going to have to reassemble it tomorrow, most likely when you're in a rush to get somewhere.

➤ If your car seat has two parts, tape the bottom with airline tape before you head off, as seats tend to dismantle.

➤ If you can, ensure your front seats are beyond the reach of your kids' feet, as they are powerless to resist the urge to kick the back of your seat.

➤ If you care about your car's condition in the future, use mats or seat covers under the car seats to catch food and bodily fluids.

➤ As per manufacturers' recommendations, always fold the extra straps away, and install the seat correctly.

PACKING FOR THE CAR

It's amazing how much extra stuff you'll need to keep your kids happy. Changes of clothes, nappies, books, toys, snacks, strollers, carriers, bottles, sippy cups – most of these things are not essential, but you'll probably pack them anyway.

There's a separate chapter in this book about packing (see page 126); this bit is solely concerned with how you're going to squeeze all this crap into your car. Packing a car can quickly become a game of Tetris, which is heaven when it provides an excuse to get out of the hotel/cabin during a morning tantrum, and hell when it's forty-five degrees and you're late to catch a ferry.

We solved a lot of problems by renting a trailer wherever we went to keep the car relatively uncluttered. Move Yourself Trailer Hire has self-service kiosks available at petrol stations around the country, so it's easy to pick them up and drop them off. Alternatively, invest in a trailer of your own.

You might be tempted to put your kids in the trailer as well, which is not only illegal, but will also get you funny looks.

Handy tips

➤ There's a lot of space on the floor beneath the legs of your strapped-up kids.

➤ Keep nappy bags and essentials within reach, so you don't have to stop on the side of the highway every five minutes to find them.

➤ A box of wipes and tissues should always be accessible, as well as a plastic bag for kids who suddenly turn a lighter shade of pale.

➤ Carry a cooler bag or esky for milk, cheese, yoghurt and anything else that needs to be kept cool, and keep it in your air-conditioned car instead of the trailer.

ENTERTAINMENT

There was a time, in the days of yore, when family entertainment in the car consisted of staring out the window with such immaculate boredom that it became positively meditative.

Today, in our on-demand world of hyper-accessible entertainment options, your kids are simply not going to put up with that shit. To

paraphrase the immortal words of Queen: They want it *all*, and they want it *now*!

The good news is that your kids will be strapped in and won't be able to do much about it anyway, although how much screaming and whining you can endure depends on the constitutions of both parents and kids.

Older kids will be more engaged and willing to participate in classic car games, interesting podcasts and, dare I say it, actual conversation with their parents.

Younger kids are more likely to request the same three songs over and over and eventually fall asleep. This is ideal at the start of a long road trip, and not so much by the end of one.

Either way, you're going to need options, preferably available and accessible through your vehicle's entertainment system.

Music

Music makes a road trip. I can still recall my mixtapes from epic drives across Scandinavia and the UK, along with the block-rocking beats that soundtracked my regular ten-hour drives home from university each year.

Children are *passionate* about music. It ignites every sub-system in their brains, and stimulates their creativity and engagement. In the mid-1990s, it

was believed that classical music actually made your kids smarter, although further research proved that a classic case of wishful thinking. These days, experts recommend exposing your kids to songs they can interact with through singing, clapping and dancing. This interactivity promotes cognitive learning, as opposed to just passive listening.

There's no bad style of music, but a variety of sounds and songs is definitely a good thing. Nursery rhymes will always be a hit with young ones, because the melodies are simple earworms, with basic words and imagery that kids can grasp and connect with. Of course, nursery rhymes can quickly drive you crazy, especially when 'Twinkle Twinkle Little Star' replays for the thousandth time. Having previously worked in the music industry, I'm determined to expose my kids to music that will, with any luck, give them an eclectic and more sophisticated taste than whatever slosh is currently in the charts.

Many of today's parents strive to do the same, queuing up the Beatles long before 'Baa Baa Black Sheep'. Some dads have boasted to me about their Led Zeppelin-loving eight year olds, and without doubt there's been progress.

Over the past five years, I've painstakingly tried and tested dozens of songs on my daughter, and put every track that ever captured her imagination on a USB stick and smartphone playlist for our long journey across Australia. Sometimes she would request the same song over and over, while other times she'd be happy to let it flow, and sometimes we simply couldn't stand listening to the playlist any longer.

Any way you do it, it's important to realise that any song that goes into heavy rotation, no matter how much you like it, will flip over to the list of songs you probably never want to hear again. Ever.

That's okay, if it will buy me three minutes of peace, I don't mind relegating 'Ob-La-Di, Ob-La-Da' to that category.

Handy tips

➤ Our kids often loved songs after seeing the music video on Youtube, especially if they were animated.

➤ Keep the songs upbeat, but have slower tunes ready to encourage sleep.

➤ Services like Spotify, Google Play and Apple Music are game changers. Search for public road trip playlists from other parents with songs that might appeal to your kids.

Recommend music for babies and infants

The Rockabye Baby! music series turns the hits of Radiohead, U2, The Cure, Led Zeppelin, The Beach Boys, Adele, Iron Maiden, Johnny Cash and many others into glockenspiel-heavy baby-friendly lullabies. Both kids loved it, and after a while, you start wondering why David Bowie didn't use more xylophone.

I'd also recommend Raffi. He's a legend in North America but not well known in Australia. Trust me, once your kids hear 'Baby Beluga', 'Down on Grandpa's Farm' and 'Little White Duck', it'll be heavy rotation time.

Recommend music for all Ages

The songs below might work for you, but this list ultimately says more about my family's taste than anything else.

Share with other parents the tunes that work for you at esrockingkids.com/music

- '1234' – Feist
- 'Cherry Oh Baby' – UB40
- 'Just the Two of Us' – Bill Withers
- 'Ain't No Sunshine' – Bill Withers
- 'It's Raining Again' – Supertramp
- 'Spooky' – Dusty Springfield
- 'ABC' – The Jackson 5
- 'Englishman in New York' – Sting
- Shiny Happy People' – R.E.M.
- 'Bongo Bong' – Manu Chao
- 'Gypsy' – Suzanne Vega
- 'You Can Call Me Al' – Paul Simon
- 'My Baby Just Cares for Me' – Nina Simone
- 'Beyond the Sea' – Bobby Darin
- 'Upside Down' – Jack Johnson
- 'Frog Trouble' – Mark Lanegan
- 'Let it Go' – Idina Menzel (resistance is futile)
- 'Adventure of a Lifetime' – Coldplay
- '10,000 Emerald Pools' – BØRNS
- 'HandClap' – Fitz and the Tantrums
- 'Royals' – Lorde
- 'All Star' – Smash Mouth
- 'Grapes' – Andrew & Polly
- 'A Sky Full of Stars' – Coldplay
- 'Three Little Birds' – Bob Marley
- 'Don't Worry Be Happy' – Bobby McFerrin
- 'I Sing the Body Electric' – from the film *Fame*
- 'Dy'er Maker' – Led Zeppelin
- 'All You Need is Love' – The Beatles
- 'Penny Lane' – The Beatles
- 'Yesterday' – The Beatles
- 'A Sorta Fairytale' – Tori Amos
- 'The Phantom of the Opera' – Andrew Lloyd Webber (and his other hits)
- 'Total Eclipse of the Heart' – Bonnie Tyler
- Singin' in the Rain – Gene Kelly
- 'It's Oh So Quiet' – Björk
- 'Take On Me' – A-ha
- 'Two Way Street' – Kimbra
- 'Manic Monday' – The Bangles
- 'Blackbird' – Sarah McLachlan
- 'Give Me One Reason' – Tracy Chapman
- 'Yoshimi Battles the Pink Robots' – The Flaming Lips
- 'Time After Time' – Cyndi Lauper
- 'Somewhere Over the Rainbow' – Israel Kamakawiwo'ole
- 'Shout' – Tears for Fears
- 'Radio Ga Ga' – Queen
- 'Happy' – Pharrell Williams
- 'Waka Waka' – Shakira

Games

Preschoolers don't always have the attention spans or vocabulary necessary for the classic car games. Car bingo, I-spy, Punch Buggy... our best success was playing 'Guess What Animal I Am?', which even got our two year old involved, although he always chose 'cow' and was amazed that we kept guessing it over and over.

Our five year old gravitated towards 'sasquatch', a creature she believes is absolutely real, as do twenty per cent of Americans (and I'm not even making that up).

Podcasts

An increasingly popular option for long road trips is to forego your favourite podcasts and opt for topics and productions that appeal to the kids.

Some popular podcasts for young kids include: *Story Time*, *Dream Big*, *Little Stories for Tiny People*, *SparkleCast*, *Short & Curly* and *Storynory*.

It's worth looking at the subjects before you download a particular podcast; one story we listened to, an old Japanese legend, turned pretty disturbing pretty quickly.

Once the kids fall asleep, you can return to *Freakonomics*, *Revisionist History*, *Intelligence Squared*, *99% Invisible* and *No Such Thing as a Fish*.

Screens

Some vehicles come equipped with screens, and some parents will be fine handing over a tablet to keep the kids busy.

We personally decided to limit screen time in the car and save it for when we really needed it (eating out, flights) and when the kids weren't strapped up in a car seat.

We also found it caused even more nausea than we already had to deal with.

TOILET STOPS AND LEG STRETCHES

We gave ourselves a rule: no more than two hours in the car without a stop to run about, have something to eat and burn off a little energy. Fortunately, small Australian towns have a knack for placing playgrounds and food stops close to major roads.

The only exception to our rule was if the kids were sleeping, in which case we'd drive as far as we could get before they woke up.

TAXIS

As much as we love Uber, they don't deal very well with car seats (although that seemed to depend on the state we happened to be in).

Maxi cabs were essential for airport transfers, although sometimes we had to wait *forever* before one would finally arrive (here's looking at you, Adelaide). Some taxi drivers were incredibly helpful and super patient – that is, the taxi drivers who had kids of their own and understood perfectly well what we were going through (here's looking at you, Mackay).

Some taxi drivers were straight up bastards who watched as we struggled to load up and load in (here's looking at you, Darwin).

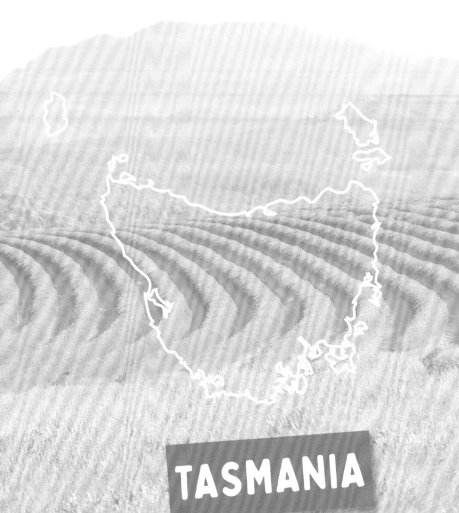

TASMANIA

THE MUSEUM
OF OLD AND NEW ART

Through the looking glass

 Age minimum: None, kids younger than eighteen years old enter free

 Open: Closed Tuesdays (except in January) and Christmas Day

 Visit: www.mona.net.au

Mona is the brainchild of a peculiar Hobart man who has the mind of a genius, the heart of a jester, the curiosity of a seven year old and the bank account of a gambling mogul. David Walsh decided to give something back to his community in the form of the weirdest, most fascinating and outrageously fun contemporary art museum in the world.

Dispensing with art-world stuffiness and employing sensorial and interactive exhibits, Mona will bewilder visitors of all ages. Exhibits include: a machine manufacturing poop; a bloated, red sports car that looks like it's melting; dozens of people singing Madonna songs on different television sets; and a two-thousand-year-old Egyptian mummy.

A neon-lit tunnel changes colours, a maze of concrete leads to an infinity room with a giant overhead mirror, a massive hallway contains hundreds of small pieces of art to form a giant snake – discovering Mona delivers a surprise and occasionally a gasp around every corner.

You might want to peek around some of those corners first before the kids do; parts of Walsh's collection are challenging, dark, disturbing and not kid-friendly, but it's easy enough to just direct little ones' attention to the next exhibit,

which might be hilarious, light and whacky.

As the largest privately funded museum in the country, Mona is built like a James Bond villain's fortress into the cliffs alongside the River Derwent. It's a twenty-minute drive from the city, or if you're up for it, you can hop aboard the camouflaged Mona fast ferry from downtown.

On arrival, we made our way along a zigzagging outdoor path to an unassuming entrance. Before we could pick up our tickets, the kids were already entranced by some of the art outside, including a large trampoline they could bounce on while ringing bells.

Once descended into the depths of the museum via an unusual elevator, we made our way through the bottom level, exploring different rooms, chambers, tunnels and galleries, all containing strange works of conceptual art. Paintings, sculptures, antiques, furniture and photographs – much of it will go over your head, figuratively and literally.

There are no explanation boards, but you do get a phone-like device with an app that describes each piece. As for the kids, prepare to say 'look but don't touch' a lot. My kids loved the *bit.fall* waterfall installation on the lower floor, which spells out words pulled from current news headlines in water. They were mesmerised to see a real-life tattooed bloke meditating

pink oversized beanbags, chased after roosters, and made some moves on a large chessboard.

Beyond the art – which stimulated conversations all week – it's the unusual spaces that left the biggest impression on our kids. A brilliant white room that robs you of your physical senses, a car jammed between two cement walls, a spaceship-like orb of metal, a tunnel to nowhere ... and that's just scratching the surface.

Combined with an overall lack of pretension and friendly Tasmanian hospitality, this full-day experience is a must for visitors of all ages to Hobart.

on a podium in perfect stillness. I suppose it is art, if you say so.

Another favourite was the *Kittens' Tea and Croquet Party*, but I wasn't going to ruin Raquel's wonder by telling her these were actual dead, stuffed cats from the nineteenth century. Some of the collection is visually bizarre and mentally challenging, sitting far beyond the insight of a toddler (although you might have to answer a lot of questions).

After a fabulous lunch at Mona's family-friendly Wine Bar, we danced to an African band playing on the outdoor stage, played with

CRADLE MOUNTAIN

A walk in the woods

 Age minimum: None, kids younger than five years old don't require a Parks Pass

 Open: Year round

 Visit: www.parks.tas.gov.au/?base=3297

Departing from Hobart, many Tasmanian family road trips head north towards Launceston. As you do, prepare to hear kids in the back pointing out shadowy shapes on the hills. These are the Midland Highway Silhouettes, with each statue depicting a scene from the region's history.

We stopped for lunch in historic Campbell Town at the heart of the state's Convict Trail. Tasmania's brutal convict history is not a subject suited for young kids, which is why they parked in a delightful cellar bookshop nearby while I read the fascinating convict histories detailed on a pathway of red bricks.

Refreshed after eating one of the better pies we found in Australia, we continued north-east on mountain roads that made us quickly regret not accompanying those pies with Travacalm.

At last we arrived at Cradle Mountain-Lake St Clair National Park, widely recognised as one of the most beautiful places in the entire country. Part of UNESCO World Heritage–protected wilderness, Cradle Mountain is a hiker's paradise, which adds a few challenges when you're with young kids who won't hike very far.

Nonetheless, there's a great selection of easy walks that showcase the region's renowned mountain beauty. Take, for example, the Dove Lake Boatshed walk. Part of the six-kilometre Dove Lake Circuit – a boardwalk that circles the lake and a must if you can do the full thing – the Boatshed stroll takes just fifteen minutes from the parking lot on a gravel and wooden trail with stunning views of the national park's iconic mountains in the background.

Another option for toddlers

is the Rainforest Walk, which is a short loop from the visitor centre at the entrance of the park. Wandering among old pine and myrtle, the payoff is the beautiful Pencil Pine Falls. There's also the Enchanted Walk, a twenty-minute family-friendly trail, although if you have small children footing it I suggest you double whatever trail time is suggested on brochures and maps.

The 1.1-kilometre Enchanted Walk continues into the rainforest, crosses Pencil Pine Creek and includes three small tunnels for the kids to crawl through, with pictures and information about local animals on the walls. Keep a lookout for

wombat burrows, although you'll probably only spot one scurrying about at dawn or dusk.

You will see distinctive button grass around Cradle Mountain, which is apparently the world's most flammable grass. Given its abundance, it's best to limit fires to barbies and pizza ovens.

We stayed in a rustic cabin at Discovery Parks Cradle Mountain, just outside the park entrance, which added to the remote wilderness feel of our visit – of truly being out in the woods.

Picking up fresh ingredients from the store at reception, we took full advantage of the pizza ovens in the communal dining area, allowing our kids to create their 'best pizza ever'. Joining us were families and travellers from around the world, drawn to Australia's most magical mountain.

DEVILS @ CRADLE

Devilishly cute

 Age minimum: None, kids younger than four years old enter free

 Open: Year round

 Visit: www.devilsatcradle.com

With all the grunts and snorts coming from the devils, I was hoping the park interpreter would have patience with the grunts and snorts coming from my two year old.

We were gathered in a room at the Devils @ Cradle conservation facility within Cradle Mountain National Park, and it was almost feeding time. Galileo wasn't nearly as hungry as the dozen or so devils salivating in their enclosures outside, but he was mimicking their throaty growls with impressive enthusiasm.

Eventually we received enough funny looks that we left the room, and missed some background about Australia's largest (living)

marsupial predator: that demonically named black-and-white ball of bat-eared fierceness. Few creatures capture a child's imagination like a devil.

The wildlife park Devils @ Cradle forms part of the nationwide Captive Breeding Program, which will ensure the devils' survival of a tragic epidemic threatening the species. Although we'd seen devils in other wildlife parks, it felt right to get to know them better in Tasmania, and the sanctuary was the ideal place to do so.

Forgoing the Day Keeper Tour, we signed up instead for the After Dark Feeding Tour, figuring the nocturnal devils would be more active. Before our disrupted debrief, we did learn that devils were once found on the mainland along with the now extinct Tasmanian tiger, and that even though one-third of Tasmania is protected wilderness, times are certainly tough for the devils.

There is still no cure for a facial tumour disease that has wiped out some eighty per cent of the devils in Tasmania since the mid-1990s. For the kids, we focused on the positive conservation efforts, but in truth they just wanted to see the sharp-toothed critters, and to hear the hissing grunts that have made the devil so famously formidable.

A night keeper entered various enclosed pens to toss or tie up meat for small packs of hungry devils. The devils made their demonic sounds as they greedily gnashed away at as much meat as they could. The kids were naturally delighted, but had a hard time understanding why they couldn't 'make nice' and pet the devils, which do resemble small dogs, albeit dogs with some of the most powerful jaws in the animal kingdom.

The night keeper explained the distinct hierarchies in each enclosure, and that once a baby devil is old enough, it will attack its own mother before heading into a life of grouchy solitude. 'And that, Raquel, is what happens when you have too much screen time,' I added.

We followed the night keeper to the quoll enclosures, where we had our first encounter with the underrated star of Australian wildlife, the country's supreme marsupial predator. Spotted-tail quolls are known to leap from trees and crush the necks of small wallabies and pademelons, just like a real-life drop bear.

Despite their deadly tactics and fierce natures, bad-ass quolls still look like fat cuddly ferrets, and outside Australia, few people even know they exist. On the other hand, and with a little help from a Warner Bros. cartoon, Tasmanian devils have attained global stardom.

Unlike other wildlife parks, Devils @ Cradle allows these grunting devils to take centre stage, even if overzealous toddlers are eager to join the performance.

BRIDESTOWE LAVENDER ESTATE

Lavender fields forever

 Age Minimum: None, all kids enter free

 Open: Year round, closed Christmas day

 Visit: www.bridestowelavender.com.au

On the advice of a parenting book – the title of which we've long since forgotten – my wife and I sometimes use colour zones to help our kids identify their moods. Things are mighty pleasant in the Blue Zone, begin to get ugly in the Yellow Zone, and God help us if we get to the Red Zone, at which point, it's wise to take shelter at the hotel bar (safely absconded to our own emotional Green Zone).

Fortunately, there is a Purple Zone, and not only is the colour pleasant to look at, but its fragrance is also calming for the soul. When added to ice-cream, it doesn't taste too bad either. Located about fifty kilometres north-east of Launceston, Bridestowe Lavender Estate is the world's largest private lavender farm, which produces some of the world's finest lavender products.

At home, we often throw a lavender sheet in the dryer to make everything smell nice and, as it turns out, throwing your kids into

260 acres of blooming lavender makes them behave nice.

Each December and January, neatly contoured rows of lavender come into bloom, attracting tens of thousands of visitors to this natural spectacle. Young kids might not engage with tours of the farm and production facility, but they'll definitely run themselves ragged between curvaceous rows of purple flowers, replenishing their energy with lavender ice-cream, fudge and infused tea at the onsite café.

For thousands of years, people have been using lavender to relieve stress, improve moods and promote sleep. Even if the smell of lavender reminds you of toilet spray, no parent travelling with young kids can afford to say no to *any* of these benefits.

Bridestowe is also famous for a purple lavender-scented stuffed bear called Bobbie. Stuffed with farm-grown lavender, the bear became a social media sensation in China, making it a particularly prized commodity. Your kids might not understand the concept of demand outstripping supply, and

there's no room for another stuffed toy, or it's too expensive, or the gift shop is sold out in the first place.

Uh-oh, looks like we might be heading into the Red Zone. In which case, grab some essential lavender oil, douse your vehicle with it for the drive home, and let the fragrance work its magic.

Check Bridestowe's website to see if the lavender flowers are in bloom, and even if they're not, rest assured the countryside aesthetics, fragrances and tastes in this peaceful Purple Zone still work their magic long after harvest.

hopefully won't tick over into the Yellow Zone when you patiently explain that you're travelling and

TASMAZIA & THE VILLAGE OF LOWER CRACKPOT

Follow the Yellow Brick Road

 Age minimum: None, kids younger than four years old enter free

 Open: Year round, closed Christmas Day

 Visit: www.tasmazia.com.au

Much like the eccentricity running amok in Hobart's Mona, the brain behind this village of mazes and miniature streetscapes has clearly found his creative Promised Land.

About forty minutes south of Devonport or north-east of Cradle Mountain, Tasmazia is nestled in a locality actually called Promised Land, a physical place where zany dreams seemingly come true.

Certainly, this proved to be the case for the dreams of the village laird, a boiler-suited Sydneysider who moved to Tasmania to pursue his passion for models and mazes.

The complex features eight different mazes, including the Great Maze, which claimed to be the world's largest at planting.

Cute jokes propel you forward, with kids ticking off landmarks on a discovery sheet picked up at the ticket office. Our toddlers had a riot following their noses through the Yellow Brick Road Maze, and we all felt a little bamboozled in the aptly named Confusion Maze.

I cover other mazes in this book, but they don't offer the Village of Lower Crackpot. Built at one-fifth scale, various houses, buildings and

world landmarks lend these streets a mischievously subversive spirit and distinct sense of humour.

Yes, that is a Monument to Whistleblowers. Yes, that sign does say: 'Children without supervision will be caught and sold as slaves'. Another: 'If you notice this notice then you'll notice that this notice is not worth noticing.'

There are weird dwellings that make little sense and others dedicated to intergalactic travel. Keep an eye out for The Principality of the Hobbits, and the Embassy of the Invisible Forces that Control

the World. It's built in good fun and all but guaranteed to delight

hot meals, and spaces to picnic too. As a bonus, the complex is also a working lavender farm, promoting that desirable Purple Zone behaviour in kids.

Brian Inder, the village laird in question, must love to see how visiting families delight in his vision. He's usually pottering about, and if you see him, he is a character well worth chatting to.

Tasmazia is a scenic drive no matter which direction you're coming from. Keep an eye out for a road sign pointing to another real-life place called Nowhere Else – an apt description, perhaps, for Tasmania in general.

open-minded families keen to engage with the scope and weirdness of it all.

There's a café on site for

EATING OUT AND DINING IN

For me, food has always been a vital component of travel. Every meal is an opportunity to savour new cuisines, and spark conversation and connection. It's a special time to sit back, relax and indulge.

When you're travelling with young children, *forget* all that. The rule of thumb is that the more expensive the restaurant, the less likely your children will eat anything of nutritional value, and the more likely they will throw a full-tilt meltdown because their crayon isn't the right shade of forest green.

• •

Allow me to dissect the formula of your typical family travel meal:

Location
A small-town restaurant with a fridge buzzing at an almost intolerable volume, which the owners don't seem to hear or mind. Air conditioning is a plus.

Enter
Family of four, two kids under five. After walking around looking for somewhere to eat for twenty minutes, if you even suggest finding somewhere else, your partner will call a divorce lawyer, or possibly, a hit man.

Highchair
Available in wood or plastic, with dried brown stains of mysterious culinary origin.

Kids' menu
All major food groups represented, including fried chicken nuggets, fried

fish, hamburgers, frozen pizza, toasted cheese sandwiches and, most importantly, chips. Apple juice is from concentrate and somehow contains both added sugar and high-fructose corn syrup.

Cost
Exactly one-third more than you'd expect to pay, but the kids' meal comes with milk or apple juice, and that sounds healthy.

Order
Nuggets for the one kid, grilled cheese sandwich for the other. Order placed immediately to get the kids fed as soon as possible.

The wait
Interminable. What are they doing? Processing the fake cheese? Looking for a bird to slaughter? Whines increase in volume and frequency until breaking point.

Length of time spent washing hands
Twenty minutes convincing your kid to do it, eight seconds when they actually do.

Length of time spent colouring books
Four minutes and twelve seconds, including one full minute of your two year old chewing on the crayon before you notice.

Length of time spent reading books
Forty-five seconds.

Length of time spent on apps on phone or tablet
No, don't do it yet, wait until it gets really bad, or until you need your hands to eat.

The food, Part One
As your kids will gladly explain in high-pitched screams to everyone within the zoning district, they now want hamburgers and pizza, not chicken nuggets and grilled cheese sandwiches. No amount of cajoling convinces them otherwise, including threats of starvation, boarding school or withholding stuffed toys at night – threats that actually amount to more punishment for you than for them. Eventually, you order the pizza and hamburger and realise that yet again, you will be dining on chicken nuggets and grilled cheese sandwiches.

Reaction of restaurant staff and other customers
A coin toss between heaven-sent patience (they have kids or grandkids) and barely contained annoyance (they don't).

The food, Part Two
By now, the food has been ignored by both kids since they have raided the crackers and fruit you carry in the snack bag and they are no longer hungry. On the plus side, they had a healthier lunch than the restaurant menu anyway, plus you can always bag their food for later, when it can be enjoyed cold and soggy, just the way no kid on Earth likes it.

The screen

Okay, use it, do it. You need a few minutes to shove that terrible food in your face so you don't become over-hungry and lose whatever patience you still cling to.

The bill

Never comes quickly enough, always costs more than anticipated and makes you question why restaurants don't put carrots, crackers and apples on their menus, because that's all kids want to eat anyway – or at least until they see them on a menu, in which case carrots, crackers and apples will become instantly toxic.

Length of ordeal

Thirty to forty-five minutes, during which time you can count on at least one toilet break, one nappy change, one smashed toy and, possibly, a broken marriage.

Remember

Sit back, relax and indulge in the cultural enrichment of new cuisines. There, isn't that better?

• •

During our journey, we ambitiously took our kids to some wonderful restaurants, especially around Melbourne's CBD and Sydney's Darling Harbour.

It was our sincere hope we'd be able to expand our kids' culinary horizons, allowing them to graduate to mild spices and unusual dishes. How proud I was when my daughter sampled crocodile, emu and kangaroo meats at the Adelaide Central Market (she drew her understandable limits at sampling citrus-nutty green ants from the Northern Territory).

'This is dill-lish-shiss!' or a hearty 'Mmmmmmm!' were not uncommon reactions. We definitely had memorable meals, although we often deployed the screen to keep the kids occupied long enough for all of us to enjoy them too.

Between eating in and eating out, it's important to treat yourselves every once in a while and budget a little extra for good food. At the end of the day, good food keeps you healthy, and, if the kids are behaving, meals can indeed be the highlight of the day.

Handy tip

We found UberEats to be a family travel revelation, combining the ease of going out with the ease of staying in.

COOKING

Wherever possible, we preferred to prepare our own meals in our holiday park cabins, Airbnbs and rental apartments. Even though we had to shop, cook and clean up, dinners are just simpler at home. We could feed the kids meals they'd actually eat, keep ourselves conveniently close to bath-tubs, toys, paper towels, toilets and ABC Kids.

Always on the move, we travelled with a box of condiments and staple ingredients, picking up fresh produce wherever we went (our kids constantly snack on fruit and vegetables, which are abundant and excellent throughout Australia).

Breakfast is particularly important and, given our schedule, was often rushed. Cereal, smashed avocado toast, Uncle Tobys porridge, Milo, eggs . . . and out the door.

Lunches were usually eaten out, hence the overflow of nuggets, sandwiches and chips, with pies coming to the rescue on more than one occasion, but wholesome home-cooked dinners could make up the health deficit. We didn't always have time to prepare elaborate meals, but we did have some easy go-to dishes, with pasta or rotisserie chicken good options in a pinch. There's much to be said for the quality of packaged meats, chicken and salads available from supermarkets these days.

In our household, Dad does the cooking, Mum does the baking and everyone cleans up. There were occasional barbecues, but unless you're travelling with your own, they're often a pain to clean.

RECIPES

Our road-tested family-friendly, easy-to-prepare dishes:

Pesto Pasta
Boil pasta, stir in bottle of pesto. Presto!
Cook time: 12 minutes.

Salmon and Roast Veggies
Roast sweet potatoes, carrots, beets, potatoes
for 30 minutes. Apply garlic and herbs to
salmon, roast for 20 minutes.
Cook time: 50 minutes.

Spaghetti Daddynese
Fry mince with onions. Add tomato sauce
from jar, dolled up with herbs, red
wine.
Boil pasta.
Cook time: 30 minutes.

Tuna Melts
Toast bread. Mix tuna and mayo.
Grate cheese. Stick in oven.
Cook time: 15 minutes.

Camembert and French Bread
Apply jam and garlic to top of camembert. Stick in oven for 12 minutes. Dip with warm bread.
Cook time: 12 minutes.

Halloumi and Salad
Coat halloumi in flour, fry on medium heat. Squeeze lemon juice over and serve hot with salad.
Cook time: 10 minutes.

If you need to make omelettes for dinner, do it. If you need to eat leftover chicken for breakfast, do it. Do whatever you need to, because any food in the belly pays dividends when you avoid hangry meltdowns in an hour or two.

OUR FAVOURITE RESTAURANTS

Mamasita, Melbourne, Victoria
This family-friendly Mexican joint served up share plates that were so good we didn't want to share them. Think street-style corn with queso-lime and chipotle mayo; barbecued octopus with hominy puree and serrano salsa; braised beef tostaditas with habanero and pickled onion; spicy lamb rib chops; and for the kids, chargrilled corn, chicken and cheese quesadillas, mouth-watering fish tacos and of course, ice-cream. Ay caramba!

Krimper Cafe, Melbourne, Victoria
Almond-crusted French toast with red wine poached pear and white chocolate and raspberry ganache for lunch? Why not?! At Krimper, Galileo gobbled up the smoked salmon scramble. Raquel highly recommends the 'Barry' smoothie. Yummy!

Top Paddock, Melbourne, Victoria

This café menu features blueberry and ricotta hotcakes, Tasmanian salmon, poached eggs and an amazing array of single-origin coffees and fresh, cold-pressed juices. The kids had creamy scrambled eggs and toast, which, judging by their empty plates, were exceptional.

Lucy Liu Kitchen and Bar, Melbourne, Victoria

When your kids are chomping down on fresh kingfish sashimi with hot mint, green chili and toasted coconut (not too spicy!) *and* Tuna Tataki with Apple Ponzu, you know they a) are hungry, b) have been eating too much fried food and c) love raw fresh seafood. The service was outstanding and our large table gave us plenty of space to share all the dishes.

The Kettle Black, Melbourne, Victoria

When I was young, juice meant sickly sweet creaming soda and raspberry cordial, mixed with one part syrup, six parts water. Today, green juice means freshly squeezed, cold-pressed kale, apple, green pepper, celery and lemon, and red juice means beet, apple, lemon, carrot and celery. The kids drank them to the bottom. This is progress.

The Barn Steakhouse, Mount Gambier, South Australia

We visited for a meaty treat to celebrate our one-month anniversary on the road with grilled porterhouse and filet mignon. The kids had fish 'n' chips (but didn't touch the fish) and steak and chips (but didn't touch the steak).

Eagle Bay Brewing Co, Margaret River, Western Australia

Here we enjoyed roasted focaccia beer bread, marinated eggplant, cashew and sun-dried tomato pesto, Korean chicken wings, Cajun prawn cakes, halloumi and roast zucchini pizza. But of course, the kids ordered fish and chips.

Holy Smoke, Pemberton, Western Australia

Feeling chipped out and as though our livers had been deep fried, we absolutely loved our taster at this arty gallery restaurant, with smoked cuts of chicken, salmon and duck, and trout and salmon pâté served with fresh fruit and salad. Absolutely scrumptious!

Mona Wine Bar, Hobart, Tasmania

Don't leave without trying God's Plate: hummus; vegetable purées; roasted, fermented and stuffed vegetables; artichokes; dukkah; labneh and crisp flatbread. There's also a deliciously rich chicken liver crème brûlée with sweet cherries, which Raquel ate like pudding.

Mures Upper Deck, Hobart, Tasmania

At one of the city's best restaurants, the kids had fish crumbed with almond and panko, along with the best chips we had in Australia. The adults had Tasmanian scallops, Pirates Bay octopus, melt-in-the-mouth salmon sashimi, oysters on the half shell served in different ways (our favourite was the Canadian), and Mures's famous line-caught trevalla, a buttery white fish caught just three days before on the restaurant's own boat!

Urban Greek, Hobart, Tasmania

Expect a family-friendly feast straight from Crete! We enjoyed warm herbed pita to dip in a *tirokafteri* (a red pepper dip) and taramas (cod's roe

with lemon and olive oil), the best dolmades we've ever had, flaming saga-naki, Piato Santorini (local salmon and white fish with fava beans, spinach, fennel, silverbeet and leek), charcoal octopus done the Greek way, three-cheese croquettes and lamb chops with lemon potatoes to make us dream of the home island.

Old Wharf Restaurant, MACq 01 Hotel, Hobart, Tasmania

Gali had fresh pesto pasta and Raquel had a juicy burger prepared in the open kitchen, while I salivated over gazpacho and grilled eggplant. Ana had fresh trout salad and oysters with a gin sorbet. This amazing hotel is full of stories for the kids to explore, too.

Rigoni's Bistro, Adelaide, South Australia

Start with an appetiser of bruschetta, served with sous-vide beef, horse-radish cream and marinated eggplant. We enjoyed crispy fried calamari, antipasto, halloumi, fried baitfish, braised lamb triangoli, sous-vide duck and pumpkin and ricotta gnocchi washed down with a bottle of Church Block from Wirra Wirra in the McLaren Vale wine region . . . mamma mia!

Muse, Canberra, Australian Capital Territory

The kids loved their morning sourdough soldiers to dip into a soft-boiled egg. Fresh Hawaiian poke bowls were something different for breakfast, along with pan-fried mushroom bruschetta with halloumi and basil pesto. It was all served with great coffee and freshly squeezed juice – now that's a way to start a day!

Agostinis in the East Hotel, Canberra, Australian Capital Territory

This is a great spot for Italian-class thin-crust pizza and perfectly al dente homemade pasta (Raquel ate a whole bowl!). I feasted on a buttery steak served on pumpkin, while Ana and Gali devoured the authentic quattro formaggi pizza.

Braza Churrascaria, Sydney, New South Wales

If you've never experienced a Brazilian restaurant, we can't recommend Braza in Darling Harbour enough. Different cuts of meat come thick and fast, expertly grilled around a fire and served with delicious traditional Brazilian staples like cassava fries, rice, beans, farofa, salads and of course, caiprinhas! Located in Darling Harbour, it's great value and a fantastic dining experience, with an authentic Brazilian thumbs up from the Mrs.

Sushi n Co., Katoomba, New South Wales

This local favourite had the best sushi we found in Australia: fresh, fast and creative, well-priced and enough to change my mind about never eating sushi outside Vancouver.

Hurricane's Grill, Sydney, New South Wales

I always visit Hurricane's when I'm in Sydney. Bountiful beef ribs, tenderloin steak, mac and cheese for the kids, all served with a smile and a view over the water. Oh, and monkey gland sauce, which has neither monkey nor glands, but is a South African barbecue sauce, which, for me, is sweetened with nostalgia.

Indiyum, Caloundra, Queensland

Our kids love their butter chicken, and who can blame them? We sampled Indian in just about every state, but we've got to raise our poppadum to this family business on the Sunshine Coast. The excellent menu descriptions (full of tasty trivia) set up the best Indian meal we ate in the country. Raquel had three helpings, which we think is a record!

The Mexican, Port Douglas, Queensland

We love restaurants that have plenty of kids' books, and this one even had a bookshop next door. The five-chilli braised beef came on a sizzling plate,

Raquel and Gali made their own tacos, the ingredients were fresh and simple, the service was outstanding and the homemade hot sauces meant business.

The Grazing Goat Cafe, Mackay, Queensland

We will be forever grateful to this family-friendly café for sneaking in our last order right before closing. We ordered high-quality homemade chicken tenders and sweet potato fries for the kids, an avocado chicken melt for Ana and a juicy Wagyu beef burger with red pepper jam for me. Plus milk-shakes, because it was that kind of day.

COFFEE N MORE at FLYNNS

KIDS MENU

I dont know..........................$5.50

CHICKEN NUGGETS AND CHIPS

I dont care...........................$5.50

CHEESE BURGER

Im not hungry.......................$5.50

HAM AND CHEESE TOASTED SANDWICH

I don't want that..................$5.50

FISH N CHIPS

Whatever............................$5.50

CRUMBED CALAMARI RINGS AND CHIPS

NEW

SOUTH

WALES

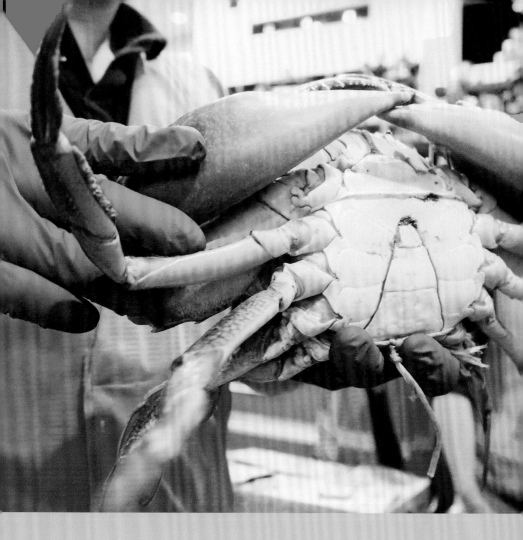

SYDNEY FISH MARKET

Something fishy

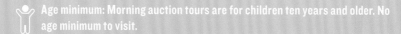

Age minimum: Morning auction tours are for children ten years and older. No age minimum to visit.

Open: Year round, but tours don't run on weekends or public holidays

Visit: www.sydneyfishmarket.com.au

Living on the coast, we eat a lot of seafood – typically the same few species as everyone else: salmon, trout, cod, tuna, shrimp, barramundi, and whatever the hell is in a fish finger these days.

When it comes to nutrition, eating fish is very good for you, especially compared to eating other meats. Unfortunately, we're not a family of anglers accustomed to baiting, hooking, dressing and cooking a fish we've plucked directly from a river or ocean (kudos to those who are).

My kids only know fish that comes neatly sliced from the super-market, frozen in boxes, pickled in jars or served as sushi. Which made our visit to the largest fish market in the southern hemisphere all the more fascinating.

Australia has the third-largest fishing zone in the world, and is home to ten per cent of all the marine creatures people eat. The variety of seafood available at the Sydney Fish Market is staggering, making a family visit sort of like exploring an aquarium – only, people come here to buy and eat fish as well as to curiously gaze at them.

Sensitive kids and future vegans might be uneasy with this seafood enterprise, but no more so than if

they visit a farm and see piglets running about (hint: piggies don't live on a farm because they're adorable).

Early-morning tours of the market's seafood auction are a must for adults, and restricted for kids aged ten and older. For younger kids, it's still well worth a more casual visit to expand their seafood horizons, learn about sustainable fishing practices and encounter so many different species. Some of these fish will be prepared fresh by various food vendors located inside the market, others will get shipped off to markets and suppliers in Asia.

Make sure the kids wear closed shoes, as there's quite a lot of water

on the ground, and keep close as trucks and workers come and go with bustling deliveries. Gazing at the fish, crabs, squid, prawns, rock

lobsters and other species in the various tanks, a few look disturbingly alien (apparently Balmain bugs inspired the aesthetics of the creature in *Alien*).

We watched a master oyster shucker crack through hundreds of fine oysters, available by the tray at a significant discount to what they'd cost in a nearby restaurant. A massive Tasmanian king crab looked like it could swallow a toddler, or at least lock one down with its sizable pincer.

Of course we had to order fish and chips from one of the vendors, and of course the kids took one bite of the deep-fried fish and focused on the chips. Personally, I loaded up on a tray of fine oysters, a delicacy my kids won't go near.

Oysters, of course, are known to be aphrodisiacs. Rest assured, slurping a dozen back in the presence of two overexcited pre-schoolers will rob this tasty mollusc of any such effect. Add another kid to this mix? Erm . . . I'll have another squeeze of lemon for now, thanks.

BONDI BEACH

Rescue me

 Age Minimum: None

 Open: Year round

 Visit: www.sydney.com/destinations/sydney/sydney-east/bondi

Kid-friendly experiences in Sydney could fill a book on their own. Taking the kids aboard the scenic ferry to Manly? Oh yeah! Taronga Zoo? Sure! Pushing a stroller around the Royal Botanic Garden to the Sydney Opera House? You betcha! Kidspace at the Australian Museum? Do it! Tackling the pylons of the Sydney Harbour Bridge Climb …? Maybe skip that one.

As for beaches, Sydney is no slouch. Locals might point you towards Bronte, Shelly, Tamarama, Balmoral and Freshwater – but only one beach dominates headlines as one of the world's great urban destinations.

You can't visit Sydney with the kids and *not* spend a few hours in the crescent-shaped bay of beautiful Bondi Beach. It's a beach for hard bodies and a beach for flabby tourists, a beach for surfers and a beach for those learning to ride a wave.

The Bondi neighbourhood has hip coffee shops and bustling bars, gourmet ice-cream parlours and cafes. Crowded as it may get, there's enough space on Bondi to accommodate masses of flesh, sizzling

under the sun. I'm always struck by the noticeable lack of umbrellas on Bondi, even when temperatures are cooking in the forties.

Families with young kids will want to beeline to the north end of the beach, where you'll find a free wading pool that's safe and shallow enough for babies to have a good splash. Nearby is the excellent Bondi Beach Playground, with shade tents and a quick dash to public toilets with change tables.

When it's time to stretch the legs, there's usually something interesting happening around Bondi, whether it's public art, marketing promotions or festivals.

Simply strolling or scootering along the promenade often delivers plenty of action as well, as it bustles with local characters, buff life-guards and lost red-faced tourists desperately in need of a sunhat.

The hardest part about a Bondi visit can be parking, so consider public transport, and perhaps avoid the beach on public holidays. Locals might scoff at putting Bondi on a list of must-do activities, but families visiting Sydney for the first time will appreciate Bondi's famed natural beauty, and unmistakable cultural significance, too.

DARLING HARBOUR

See you in the CBD

 Age minimum: None

 Open: Year round

 Visit: www.darlingharbour.com

BLUE MOUNTAINS

It's a scenic world

 Age minimum: None

 Open: Year round

 Visit: www.scenicworld.com.au

The Greater Blue Mountains Area is a UNESCO World Heritage site that covers 10,000 square kilometres below a hazy, distinctively blue sky, attributed to the dense forest of eucalyptus and plants you'll find nowhere else on the planet.

We were excited to leave the choking CBD traffic behind us for some mountain action, only to discover that it's not easy escaping Sydney's traffic, and the Blue Mountains are not at all like the mountains we know back in Canada.

Instead of soaring peaks, our two-hour drive gradually elevated us onto an escarpment overlooking the beautiful Jamison Valley, framed by sandstone cliffs. Pulling into a lookout called Echo Point,

we learned the mountains are the second most-visited tourist attraction in Australia, after the Sydney Opera House.

This is largely due to their proximity as a day trip from Sydney, and the beauty of the Three Sisters – three unusual rock formations with an enduring Indigenous Dreamtime legend. The 800-step Giant Stairway to the valley floor and ninety-minute hike that follows is a wonderful adventure – if you didn't have very young kids.

If you do, I'd suggest you head to Scenic World, a former coalmine that has become the country's most visited privately owned attraction. Before you enter, you should know

that a gondola has cars attached to a cable that circulate continuously, whereas a tramway has one large car that shuttles back and forth, and a funicular uses cables to pull a carriage up and down a steep incline.

Scenic World has two of these three, and one of them happens to be the world's steepest passenger railway. The kids are in for a treat.

Scenic World is a very slick machine. We immediately headed to the Skyway, a 720-metre gondola with a glass floor that let us stare down at a ravine and waterfall 270 metres below. With a great view of the Three Sisters, we took a short stroll to a lookout over the valley, and returned across the ravine for our next scenic and ridiculously steep ride.

The Scenic Railway tram

allowed us to adjust our seating for a sixty-four-degree incline, which of course we had to try. It's like riding a slow and steady 310-metre long rollercoaster, using your knees to support yourself. At this point, our toddler was getting a little unnerved, much like the adults. Our five year old was whooping all the way.

We took the round trip back up to hop on the Scenic Cableway, another large tramway that takes visitors 545 metres down to the valley floor. A wooden boardwalk loop let us tramp through the immaculate forest, where we encountered unusual ferns, apple gums, sassafras and lilli pilli trees, and the distinct calls of nature's ventriloquist, the lyre bird.

We didn't take the full 2.4-kilo-metre boardwalk loop (kids!) and

headed instead to the entrance of the original coalmine, where we learned more about the region's history and spent too much time playing with a bronze statue of a horse (kids!).

Conveniently, this spot is also close to the bottom of the Scenic Railway, so we got a third opportunity to feel gravity lurch us forward on the world's steepest rail ride. At this point, Galileo put his foot down and his lungs out to let us know that a) he hadn't napped and b) the sensation of plummeting 310 metres down a ravine can be endured once, maybe twice, but three times? Nuh-uh.

All in all, the Blue Mountains made for a busy, beautiful and scenic day trip from Sydney,

although you might want to spend the night in Katoomba and avoid that Sydney traffic just a little bit longer.

TREETOPS ADVENTURES

Out of our trees

 Age minimum: Three years for the TreeTops Adventure Park, twenty-five-kilogram minimum for the Crazy Rider

 **Open:** Year round, closed Christmas Day or in the event of high winds or lightning

 Visit: www.treetops.com.au

Just over two decades ago, ziplines emerged as a fun and safe family adventure that allowed us to appreciate the forest canopy as never before. Today zipline operations are everywhere – from theme parks to jungles – and I've found the quality of the experience depends much on the location and the people you're sharing the experience with. Much like travel in general.

Always on the hunt for something different, the grapevine buzzed with news of a treetop rollercoaster located along the Central Coast of New South Wales. Taking its cue from ziplines, it's an entirely original and unique Australian concept that took four years, two thousand hours of research and ten thousand hours to build.

Picture a flying fox that allows riders to not only zip between trees, but also through, alongside, and around them. Riders are safely and comfortably attached to a permanent rail, much like a human rollercoaster, and gravity pretty much does the rest.

The result is the kilometre-long TreeTop Crazy Rider Xtreme, located in the Ourimbah State Forest. Attached to an established high ropes course and with the blessing of the Forestry Corporation of NSW, it is billed as the world's first, fastest, highest and longest treetop rollercoaster.

If your kids weigh fewer than twenty-five kilograms and can't partake in the 360-degree loops of the rollercoaster, fear not. A

Treetop Adventure Park is on site, consisting of a ropes course for kids aged three to nine years.

After watching her mum swoop through the forest on the treetop rollercoaster, Raquel was harnessed up and put on the lowest level of the adventure park. Figuring she wouldn't last more than a few minutes, she surprised us all by going, and going, and going, graduating over increasingly difficult and elevated challenges.

At one point, I found myself humming the theme song for *Indiana Jones* in encouragement. Raquel closed her eyes and steadied her knees, saying, 'I can do this!' We'd been travelling for three months at this point, and if we needed any evidence as to how the road had given our kids strength, self-confidence and a sense of adventure, here it was.

My daughter continued to successfully navigate obstacles built for kids twice her age and height, completing the course with the same glow of satisfaction and buzz we had from the treetop rollercoaster. Soon enough, she'll be heavy enough to hop in the harness and nothing will stop her screaming through the trees.

IRUKANDJI SHARK & RAY ENCOUNTERS

Ray hugs and shark kisses

 Age minimum: None, kids three years old and under enter free

 Open: Year round, closed Christmas Day

 Visit: www.sharkencounters.com.au

Sharks and stingrays get a bad rap. Although horses and kangaroos kill far more people than sharks do each year, sharks get ravaged in the press, and remain the apex predator in our popular imagination. Believe me, if sharks actually wanted to eat people, nobody would be crazy enough to go surfing.

As for stingrays, well, there's the Steve Irwin thing. The reality is that most animals are harmless if you leave them alone and don't give them cause to attack. Not that I'd go swimming outside a cage with a great white, or hop out of a Land Rover to pet a lion, which would provide as compelling a reason as

any for these animals to attack.

Despite the low numbers of attacks and sharks' vital importance to the marine ecosystem, about 100 million are killed each year. Husband and wife team Ryan and Lia Pereira are working hard to change our perception of these creatures.

Irukandji Shark & Ray Encounters is devoted to busting harmful myths about these fascinating creatures, and educating visitors about marine conservation. With more than 200 animals, our family couldn't wait to slip on wetsuits and get into the pools with curious southern eagle rays,

friendly Port Jackson sharks, cuddly bluespotted stingrays, massive smooth rays and three-metre-long tawny nurse sharks.

Okay, the kids were freaked out at first; some of these creatures are bigger than them after all, but after a while my daughter warmed up to the cuddles of a huge, curious smooth ray (yes, the same species that caused the tragic death of Steve Irwin).

Our guide Lia did a fantastic job of educating us about the creatures she treats with all the love of a shark-ray mumma.

The indoor facility itself is a little rough around the edges, with

the feel of two young people doing their best to make a difference despite intense operating costs. Given the challenges of operating a tourist attraction with creatures that inspire fear and awe as the drawcard, Irukandji looks like it would make a great setting for a movie or TV show.

There are three main pools: a little pool for the smaller kids to stand and feed the rays, a larger pool where you can get a bird's-eye-view photo of yourself surrounded by swirling rays, and another adjacent large pool where nurse sharks swim.

There are also touching pools and various displays to educate kids about the different creatures. Wet suits are provided by the facility, and the utmost care is taken to ensure the animals are healthy and looked after.

Ryan and Lia's devotion and passion for their animals is inspiring, and the lessons they impart to visitors of all ages are vital. In the words of David Attenborough: 'No one will protect what they don't care about; and no one will care about what they have never experienced.'

TOBOGGAN HILL PARK

Apply the brakes

 Age minimum: None, kids three years old and under enter free. Kids younger than seven years old ride the toboggan free (accompanied by an adult)

 Open: Year round with restricted hours May to August, closed Christmas Day and Boxing Day

 Visit: www.tobogganhillpark.com

Like many a family travelling up the coast of New South Wales, we spent a few days in Port Stephens to enjoy the beaches, local attractions and Oaks Pacific Blue Resort's river-like circular pool, which they claim is the longest pool in the country.

While the kids went on their brave, floatie-supported excursions around the pool, I explored the largest coastal sand dunes in the southern hemisphere on an all-terrain vehicle (ATV). Sand Dune Adventures are fantastic, but the minimum age for participating is twelve years.

Once the kids were pooled out, we drove around the corner to

Toboggan Hill Park for some child-friendly adventures. With its range of outdoor and indoor activities, the park is perfect for young kids. We kicked things off with the namesake toboggan, a one-kilometre metal track that descends three hundred metres with eleven bends.

With the kids seated between our legs, we hitched our toboggans onto the rope tow, slowly made our way up the hill, and effortlessly slid onto the track. There's no steering wheel, just a simple brake lever to slow down the toboggan.

Kids over eight can pilot their own toboggan, but safely tucked between Mum and Dad's legs, our younger ones were enthralled.

After conquering the giant maze, we had more fun than we'd like to admit in the Splash Down, firing water balloons at each other with a slingshot catapult. Just a few days before, we'd had a long discussion with the kids about plastic waste and why balloons are so bad for the environment, and then, *pow*, we were destroying dozens of balloons in an activity park because . . . well, they were belly laughing every time I got nailed by a water balloon. Parenting . . . it's complicated.

The indoor attractions are perfect for rainy days, or to escape the sun. Toboggan Hill offers something called a hot ice rink, where you rent normal ice skates but slide on a sort of silicon surface. It's not ice, and it's not hot, but it is weird.

There's also a sizable jumping castle, kiddie bumper cars, a merry-go-round and various carnival/arcade games. The climbing wall was a particular hit, with our five year old once again showing her steely determination to get to the top.

There's also a picnic area and food kiosk on site. Toboggan Hill Park was a fun afternoon for the kids, allowing us to sit back at the resort pool with a cold beer and the feeling that, despite the plastic balloon fail, we had excelled at our parenting duties. At least until tomorrow.

HUNTER VALLEY GARDENS

Smell the roses

 Age minimum: None, kids three years old and younger enter for free

 Open: Year round, closed Christmas Day

 Visit: www.huntervalleygardens.com.au

'Just lovely!' Several old ladies were in a delightful tizz as our train of passenger carts ambled along eight kilometres of pathway through Australia's largest show garden. Flowers were blooming, roses were budding, the sky was a rich blue and horny gnomes were chasing fairies.

The thirty-five-minute intro-ductory train ride into the Hunter Valley Gardens was lovely, much like the Hunter Valley itself. The country's oldest wine region has rolling hills of vineyards, resorts, golf courses and hot air balloons floating in the early morning breeze.

Life looks pretty sweet here, especially if you have a green thumb. It took four years and forty gardeners to craft the Hunter Valley Gardens, one of the region's most popular attractions. As the train worked its way through the exquisite Japanese, Oriental, Rose, Formal and Indian Gardens, it was pretty obvious why.

We hopped off and returned by foot to our favourite spots – the Moongate, the pagoda with shadowy koi swimming the pond and the Sunken Garden. It was a warm day and the kids took their sweet time until they saw the Storybook Garden, which had an effect similar to force-feeding them twenty-three Cherry Ripes.

Various fairy-tales were brought to life through life-size sculptures, allowing the kids to

visualise Humpty Dumpty, Alice in Wonderland, Jack, Jill, Hansel and Gretel (with the house of sweets doubling as toddler-friendly toilets). During special events at Easter, Christmas and school holidays, the gardens operate a towering twenty-five-metre Ferris wheel, flying swing chair, thirty-five-metre-long super slide and life-size dinos and dragons.

Back home in Vancouver, we live close to a century-old merry-go-round that happens to be the fastest in North America, and spins so fast you feel wind in your hair. The Hunter Valley Gardens has a far gentler version, although I was interested to learn the gardens themselves were inspired by the Butchart Gardens on Vancouver Island.

By midday the kids were run out, and other than the Storybook Garden, the refined natural setting does lend itself more to slow romantic walks, or high teas with tittering old ladies.

Unlike the Royal Botanic Garden in Sydney, the Blue Mountains Botanic Garden and the Australian Botanic Garden in Mount Annan – all of which are free – Hunter Valley Gardens has an entrance fee. It's not cheap planting and maintaining 250,000 annuals, 6000 trees, 500,000-plus shrubs and more than a million ground covers.

Still, if you're staying in the Hunter Valley for a few days, or choose to make the two-hour drive out of Sydney, it's undoubtedly one of the region's highlights, a lovely day out in a lovely part of New South Wales.

BYRON BAY

The sound of sunshine

 Age minimum: None

 Open: Year round

 Visit: www.visitbyronbay.com

'I love your curls!' With her mop of untamed locks, my daughter hears this a lot when we travel – but usually not from famous American musicians, and certainly not after we'd been listening to said musician on the drive up the coast to Byron Bay. Michael Franti was in town, along with plenty of other amazing talents, for the annual Byron Bay Bluesfest.

Each Easter, Australia's most iconic beach town swells to bursting. A lot of people wandered between Jonson and Middleton streets – surfers, hippies, backpackers, yuppies, yoga bunnies – but I suppose that's usually the case. Byron has a vibe all of its own: relaxed, alternative,

arty, surfy, organic.

When we tried to book somewhere months in advance, we couldn't find a place to stay over this busy long weekend, and so had to drive into Byron from our Airbnb in the satellite village of Lennox Head.

The traffic was horrendous and, admittedly, I was sceptical about whether visiting Byron at such a time would be worth it, until we arrived at Main Beach. Crowds were lounging on the cut grass in Dening Park, drinking wine from discreet coolers, listening to far-above-average buskers.

After we navigated the bumper-to-bumper traffic and limited parking, the kids ran onto

the massive beach like tigers released from a cage. There were families everywhere, and the town is known to be particularly kid-friendly.

Legs stretched, tummies inevitably began to growl. I never noticed the overlap between backpackers in search of cheap and fast pizza and families in search of cheap and fast pizza, but here it was – separate worlds united by a decent thin crust slice of margherita on Jonson Street.

Backpackers in Byron can party all night, surf all day, or wake up before dawn to hike the four-kilometre lighthouse loop. If they time it right, they'll catch the first sunrise in Australia from the whitewashed nineteenth-century Cape Byron Lighthouse.

Families will likely opt for a car to catch the sensational sunset from the same lighthouse. Good luck and deep respect to those parents who wake up the same kids who kept them up all night to see a sunrise.

With the traffic, it took a few long loops before I could find parking near the lighthouse itself. Tip: always drop off a partner and the kids *before* looking for parking, especially when you'll have to drive up and down a busy narrow road on a cliff.

The sunset was magical. Here we were at the easternmost point in Australia recalling that several months ago, we had been sailing off the westernmost point in Australia, also at sunset. I'd call that an accomplishment, but driving to the top of the hill without a kid barfing in the back seat is also an accomplishment.

For kids over five, I recommend joining Go Sea Kayak for a guided tour into the bay in search of the resident dolphins or migrating whales, between June and November. If you don't see any, you can paddle again with them for free!

Both the town and region are blessed with wonderful beaches, and everyone will have their favourite. The Pass or Wategos, Main or Clarkes? Personally, we learned long ago that the best family beaches are close to amenities, and aren't too crowded or too difficult to access.

Parents know that when young kids have had enough, they've had enough. So it was time to hit a Sunday market, visit a café or restaurant, hang out at the fine Apex Park Playground or people watch around town. Which is how we bumped into Michael Franti on the street.

Both our wives were shopping inside the same funky boutique store, but Franti didn't have a curly-haired kid to keep him company. Franti radiated good vibes, and I guess cosmic synergy was firing for us to have bumped into one of our favourite musicians that afternoon. Or perhaps that was just the magic of Byron Bay.

CRYSTAL CASTLE

Amplifying energy

 Age minimum: None, kids four years old and younger enter free

 Open: Year round, closed Christmas Day, Boxing Day and Good Friday

 Visit: www.crystalcastle.com.au

Did you know that mazes were originally designed to lose yourself within, while labyrinths were designed as spaces to find yourself through introspection?

Think about that when your kids are running around screaming inside the labyrinth at Crystal Castle, wired on whatever frequencies the biggest geodes in the world are transmitting to their juice-soaked brains.

Crystals are known to amplify energy, just like apple juice, ice-cream and popular phrases like 'It's time for bed, kids!' Located about twenty-five minutes' drive from Byron Bay, the Crystal Castle and Shambhala Gardens display some of the world's most spectacular crystals, arranged in a beautiful environment that attracts tourists, healers, seekers and finders from around the world.

On site are various spiritual attractions, including a World Peace Stupa blessed by the Dalai Lama, energy portals, meditation nooks and giant stone Buddha statues.

On one big tree, people write wishes on paper and tie them to the branches. I asked my daughter what wish she wanted to make. She said she wished to be a knight. 'A knight-ess, and why not add "make everyone in the world happy" while we're at it?' I added.

jaws hit the floor when we entered the Enchanted Cave. It's a massive egg-shaped hollow rock that just happens to be the largest amethyst geode ever discovered.

We entered the cave to see a galaxy of crystals sparkling with light and brilliant colour. Discovered in Uruguay and shipped to Australia at great expense, the Enchanted Cave alone is worth the admission price.

From here, we marvelled at a spinning 310-kilogram orb of rose quartz, posed between amethyst geodes and strolled through the airy (and excellent) onsite cafe to

Unlike Macadamia Castle, another family-friendly attraction not far away, Crystal Castle does not resemble a castle at all. The attractions are spread around the gardens, adding to a sense of discovery as we walked along the paths, unsure of what we'd find next.

Behind the stupa, we removed our shoes for a reflexology pebble walk, surrounding a four-tonne chunk of rose quartz. The kids didn't have the patience to follow the rules of the Damanhur energy portal (which apparently connects to some hotspot in Italy) but their

see the towering Crystal Guardians framing the lush valley below. Here, a staff member led a puja ritual, explaining the history, power and purpose of the world's tallest quartz geode, split into two pieces to allow visitors to recharge between them.

We continued into the gardens on the Buddha Walk, crossing statues of various eastern deities. There were a fossilised rock from Madagascar, a bamboo forest and plenty of other spots that would have been nice to meditate at if the kids hadn't been beelining for the crystal shop to choose their own crystal keepsake.

A friendly staff member advised the kids to choose the crystal that spoke to them. I advised them to choose a crystal that didn't cost more than a couple of bucks. My daughter chose a stone that she felt would help her be brave, while my son chose a rose quartz, which apparently amplifies love, giving him permission to shower us with his wet kisses.

It's likely your enjoyment of Castle Crystal will depend on your affinity for crystals and cosmic energy (it's no accident the castle is located so close to Byron Bay). As someone on the fence, there's no denying it's a unique space with some very special attractions, and a fascinating family destination to find yourself – or lose yourself – in.

MONEY MATTERS

Let's not beat around the bank card; travel is not cheap. Especially in Australia. However you choose to take on your family trip – motorhome, resorts, hallucinogens – costs must be considered.

When someone asks me, 'How much would it cost to travel to [somewhere] for two weeks?' my answer is always the same: it all depends on your choices.

What is your mode of transport? How many and what type of activities do you want to do? What kind of restaurants will you eat in, and what will you order at those restaurants? Are you flying in economy (likely) or in a private jet? (Invites always welcome.) Are you investing in serious luggage, or travelling with shopping bags? Do you have champagne taste with a beer budget and prefer prix-fixe to meat pies?

There are families from all income groups on the road, because the desire to travel will always transcend the socio-economic divide. Any family can do it, especially with goals and expectations to suit your particular situation.

I know a family where the parents took a year off to travel after fifteen years spinning in a corporate hamster wheel, and since the hamster wheel waited for their return, money was no object. I've met families who sold *everything* to travel when the opportunity presented itself.

. . . .

My own adventures were inspired by sound advice from my grandfather. He once told me it was his dream to travel the world, and he always thought he would when he retired. But by the time he did, he was too old, too unhealthy and too sidetracked with responsibilities. 'Do it while you can!' he told me, and so I did. When your kids start school, it's going to be a lot harder to take six months off for the Big Lap, and if you're waiting for retirement, well, you might be waiting for a very long time.

Simply put: I can't answer how much this will all cost. And it might sound like a cop-out, but I wouldn't have been able to afford our own family adventure if I didn't do what I do.

As a professional travel writer, it's taken me well over a decade to build a career that allows me to ask for support from companies and organisations. Before you think about starting a blog and pitching to companies to offset your expenses, know that activities and organisations are inundated with such requests, daily.

Without an actual audience (more than just say, your mum and drinking buddies) or a credible reputation, you're going to work very hard without going very far. Still, there are some nifty ways to save money on the road.

MAKE YOUR OWN MEALS

Home cooking is more affordable, manageable and given what's on the menu for kids at most restaurants (see p 220), a lot healthier, too. It also stretches into leftovers and lunches. Our padded meal budget was about $100 a day, and food was *by far* our biggest expense.

FREE EXPERIENCES

Google 'Best Free things to do in [insert place]' and the oracle will present you with plenty of options. As you'll notice in the activities listed in this book, many excursions are free for very young kids.

PRICE ALERTS

If you're flying, do your research and watch out for cookies that let the airlines know you're looking. Use different browsers, clear your cache if you're monitoring a flight, or set price alerts.

AVOID HIGH SEASON

Young kids don't lock you into the rigid school holidays, and different states have different holiday times. Accommodation prices drop significantly in shoulder or off-season periods, and destinations are significantly less crowded too. It is also possible to negotiate a mid-term holiday with schools and teachers. This usually involves a bit of holiday homework that you may or may not diligently enforce.

LONG-TERM SAVINGS

Think ahead. Start a travel fund when your kids are babies, which might include a monthly automatic deduction into an investment account that will appreciate as your children grow. After a few years, you might have saved up more than you think. Ditto for their education, but I'll leave that sort of advice to *The Barefoot Investor*.

COVER YOUR COSTS

Just as we were using Airbnb for accommodation on the road, we also listed our home on Airbnb to cover our mortgage and other costs. We had four families stay in our home, and the whole experience worked out perfectly for all concerned.

STOP BUYING STUFF

Once you start travelling, you'll be amazed at how little you actually need as opposed to how much you have. Clothes, electronics, toys, gadgets . . . everything can be distilled into the must-haves and the why-haves. You can always pick up anything you need on the road.

SELL EXCESS STUFF

The second car? That old guitar you haven't picked up since you gave up dreaming of being a rock star? Books, CDs, toys, clothes . . . think of each sale as contributing to another lifelong memory.

BUDGET

You need to keep a grip on expenses. We're not numbers people, but we still logged all our expenses to make sure we stayed on track. We also included line items for booze and miscellaneous items, and padded it generously.

ON THAT NOTE, LAY OFF THE BOOZE

Beer and wine adds up, and you've got to ask yourself, is it worth it? Yes, of course! Just go with whatever is in the bargain bin, because after a long day dealing with kids on the road, alcohol is about the point, not the label.

GET OFF MAIN STREET

Packing picnics saved us a bundle, and restaurants tend to get cheaper the further away you are from main tourist hotspots. Look online for deals and special offers.

DRIVE THE SPEED LIMIT

When that cop pulled us over and gave us a speeding ticket in the butthole of Western Australia, it burned. Especially because I *was* driving the speed limit, just not the ten kilometres an hour slower that was required when you're pulling a trailer (a law that nobody told me about). Another strong recommendation: pay the parking fees.

CREDIT CARDS/POINTS

Loyalty programs dangle all sorts of benefits, and seldom deliver when you actually need them, but they can help with flights and hotels if used with cunning and diligence.

TAP WATER

Australia is blessed with clean drinking water. Save on the overpriced juices and unhealthy soft drinks, and instead carry water bottles. Any restaurant licensed to serve alcohol must provide free water, so take advantage of it.

BACKPACKERS

Many backpackers and hostels welcome families, providing special fami-ly-sized rooms. It's worth doing your research on this one, though, as you'll want to make sure you're not sharing a bathroom with overly boisterous Canadians from Dildo, Newfoundland.

FREE TRANSPORT

Australia's major cities offer free transport options in the CBD, including tram routes in Adelaide and Melbourne, train and bus routes in Perth and Route 555 in Sydney.

ACTIVITIES VS. ATTRACTIONS

Although many of the ideas in this book do cost money, not everything you do when you travel requires an entry ticket. Consider parks, beaches, walks, playgrounds, marinas, business districts, drives, lookouts, events and festivals.

STAY WITH FRIENDS

Believe me, there's nothing your mates will appreciate more than you showing up at their door with your two not-quite-potty-trained kids. The truth of this statement depends entirely on whether your mates *also* have not-quite-potty-trained kids, and somewhere to put you up for a couple nights.

AUSTRALIAN

CAPITAL

TERRITORY

QUESTACON

iParent

 Age minimum: None, kids under four years old enter free

 Open: Year round, closed Christmas Day

 Visit: www.questacon.edu.au

You know you've struck activity gold when your kids are happy to spend an hour in the entrance foyer. Raquel and Galileo were glued to a mechanical humanoid named RoboQ, who happens to sing songs and perform scenes from famous plays and movies.

While the cultural context of these flew over the kids' heads, RoboQ's mechanical pistons and responsive actions had them applauding for more. It was the perfect introduction to Questacon: the National Science and Technology Centre, built to make science fun, relevant and interactive – for kids and the rest of us, too.

Questacon was founded in 1980 as a volunteer-led project by the

Australian National University to inspire scientific education, and has since grown into the country's largest science centre. Half the cost of this appropriately modern building was covered by the Japanese government and business community as part of the 1988 Australia–Japan Bicentennial Project.

The fascination with how things work transcends all languages, including the language of toddlers who can't string sentences together. RoboQ needed some oil maintenance, so I finally managed to usher the kids into the Mini Q section, conveniently located off the lobby. With different areas set up for Space Play, Water Play, Active Play, Sensory Play and Role Play, the kids

would have happily spent all day there, too.

Everything is infused with educational value, from dressing up in lab coats to redirecting objects on water, making it all time well spent. With so much to offer kids under six, the price of admission is worth it for Mini Q alone, and we *still* hadn't gone beyond the entrance level. There's even a Quiet Space for napping.

There are seven other interactive galleries and more than two hundred more exhibits to explore. The different galleries are handily categorised by age, so we headed to the Fundamental gallery next,

which is all ages. Over a dozen exhibits show the workings of classic scientific concepts, and the kids gravitated to the light harp, falling magnet and pendulum snake.

Fearing the kids would treat the centre's impressive interior ramp like a playground feature, we took the elevator to our next all ages gallery, which explored the world of colour.

The two-dozen exhibits in the dark room allowed us to compare our perceptions, play with different colour contraptions and see how colour is viewed differently by different species. At this point,

With so much to see, my wife and I took turns with the kids so we could explore all the galleries, including the high-energy activities in the Energy@Q gallery. Don't leave without braving the Free Fall, and kids will love the Rototron.

By now you've probably realised that Questacon is best enjoyed over more than one visit, which is perfectly fine, because underrated Canberra definitely shares that quality too.

your kids will probably be tired and overstimulated, which is a fine reason to pop across the street to the National Library for a yummy burger break in the lobby restaurant.

The kids were excited to return to the Moon and Awesome Earth galleries, which is encouraging when your son is named Galileo. We felt the ground shake in the Earthquake Lab, watched a tornado form, and waited anxiously for a Tesla Coil to generate some shocking magic in the Lightning Cage, which activates every fifteen minutes and might scare the younger kids.

loring the solar system and beyo

CANBERRA DEEP SPACE COMMUNICATION COMPLEX

Reach for the stars

 Age minimum: None

 Open: Year round, closed Christmas day

 Visit: www.cdscc.nasa.gov

If we are just tiny atoms in an unfathomably large universe, spare a thought for the toddlers who don't even reach our hips. They must feel very small indeed, although that shouldn't stop them having very big dreams.

We named our son Galileo not only because it rolls off the tongue like a great lyric, but also for the man credited as the father of modern science, astronomy and physics. Bearing in mind that neither of his parents are scientifically inclined in any way, it's a very big name for our little Gali to live up to, so I figured we might as well get him started thirty-five kilometres south-west of Canberra.

The Canberra Space Centre is the visitor centre of NASA's Deep Space Communication Complex, one of only three such centres in the world. The others are located in remote sites in California and Spain, exactly 120 degrees in longitude apart. Several giant and striking antennae receive data from the furthermost man-made objects in the universe, including the Voyager satellites, and provide cutting-edge data in the fields of radio astronomy, interferometry, earth dynamics and sky surveys.

I also don't know exactly what that means, which is why there's a handy visitor centre to explain it all, along with the remarkable history of space travel. Many people don't know that NASA is a government-funded agency that makes its data available to the public. It is

not like the US National Security Agency (NSA), and is not shrouded in secrecy, like the mysterious Pine Gap military base (which the NSA operates outside Alice Springs).

This means that, other than Christmas Day, anyone can just show up at the Deep Space Communication Complex in rural Tidbinbilla to see those massive antennae, and what's more, it's free.

You'll feel like you're stepping into the pages of a science-fiction novel, especially with the low hum of data arriving in faint whispers from billions of kilometres away, represented on flat-screen TVs. The data is automatically sent to NASA's Jet Propulsion Laboratory, and the facility is entirely funded out of NASA's budget, although Australian engineers, programmers and staff operate and manage it.

Australia, it turns out, has been instrumental in our attempts to understand the universe. We learned that images of Neil Armstrong's historic moon walk were first captured by a twenty-six-metre dish that is still in the facility, and that the sixty-four-metre dish in Parkes, New South Wales came into action a little later (a fact, along with many others, missing in the movie *The Dish*).

'Why are the satellite dishes so big?' asked my daughter, to which our guide responded: 'Because, to hear very soft sounds from very far away, we need very big ears.'

We looked at the WALL-E-like real-life replica of the Mars Rover, popped our heads into an actual astronaut space suit, and looked at various display exhibits. Many years ago, I visited the Russian Cosmonaut Training Centre outside Moscow, and discovered just how big the gap is between science fiction and reality. I didn't expect duct tape and printer ports on actual rocket ships, and if you're expecting *Star Trek* high-tech wizardry here, you'll be similarly disappointed.

Still, the visitor centre is clearly a labour of love, presented by folks who are immensely enthusiastic about the universe beyond our world. And you can't fault the star attraction or, more accurately, the moon attraction: a single piece of priceless moon rock. It's not made of cheese, although you might find some cheesecake at the onsite Moon Rock Café, to be enjoyed with coffee and a view of the largest steerable antenna in the southern hemisphere.

While space-loving parents may want to go down the centre's black hole of knick-knacks (check out the info cards about the faked Apollo moon landing), kids can play spaceships and aliens in the small playground outside. On the beautiful late-afternoon drive back to Canberra we were all inspired by this glimpse of our place in the universe. Galileo fell sound asleep, deep space lulling him into a deep sleep, likely dreaming of the stars.

TIDBINBILLA NATURE RESERVE

Wild outside the capital

 Age minimum: None, kids under four years old enter free

 Open: Year round, closed Christmas Day

 Visit: www.tidbinbilla.act.gov.au

Connecting your kids to outer space is not the only reason to make the forty-five-minute scenic drive from Canberra to Tidbinbilla.

Not far from the Deep Space Communication Complex is Tidbinbilla Nature Reserve, a 54.5-square-kilometre protected park located within a large valley. As part of the Australian Alps National Parks, it's an ideal place to get away from Canberra's not-so-frenetic urban life, and connect with native bush and wildlife.

There are twenty-two marked trails, ranging from short fifteen-minute jaunts (ideal for the kids) to six-hour long treks (best to leave the kids behind). The kids of course will be less concerned with the bush and more enthusiastic about the animals.

The reserve has an endangered species breeding program for three critically endangered Aussie creatures: the northern corroboree frog, the southern brush-tailed rock wallaby and the eastern bettong.

Various tours with wildlife officers, offered particularly throughout the summer months, connect visitors with these and other animals. In 2003, a bushfire tragically devastated almost the entire park, with just a handful of protected species saved.

Today, healthy populations of kangaroos, potoroos, possums, wombats, echidnas, emus, lyrebirds, platypuses and other native favourites have bounced back. A

boardwalk, but the freakiest of all Australian mammals remained stubbornly elusive. We had more luck on the easy 700-metre-long Koala Path, where we spotted koalas, poteroos and wallaroos.

That afternoon, we saw many of the 160 bird species found in the reserve, as well as long-necked turtles and various lizards. The variety and abundance of animals impressed our little guys, who quickly learned that seeing animals in the wild is a very different experience to seeing them in a wildlife park.

Accommodation on site is limited to educational groups, although there is a historic yet basic homestead to rent if you've got your camping things with you, and pop-up family wilderness camps run in the summer.

Visitors are charged by the carload, which is great value for families. Together with the Deep Space Communication Centre, a full day trip to Tidbinbilla should keep the whole family smiling, capped off with a beautiful drive back to the city.

friendly wildlife officer showed us around the sanctuary's wetlands, consisting of five ponds beside the Tidbinbilla River.

We kept our eyes peeled for platypuses along the stroller-friendly 1.1-kilometre

NATIONAL DINOSAUR MUSEUM

Old Macdonald had a triceratops

 Age minimum: None, kids under four years old enter free

 Open: Year round, closed Christmas Day

 Visit: www.nationaldinosaurmuseum.com.au

Kids get exposed to terrifying yet deeply alluring images of dinosaurs at a very young age, and I often wonder if they believe dinosaurs are as real as cows, horses and sheep.

We have little plastic farmyard toys, and little plastic dinosaur toys, so why wouldn't they exist in the same universe? Hundreds of millions of years of evolutionary history and the finer points of palaeontology typically go over the heads of preschoolers, but hopping atop a life-size baby T-Rex and hearing the roar of a robotic dinosaur is a different matter.

This is why there's an understandable buzz of excitement and fear as the kids enter the National Dinosaur Museum through the replica jaws of a T-Rex. Inside is the largest permanent dinosaur collection in the country, making this museum one of the more popular family attractions in Canberra.

Kids can touch imitations of scaled and feathered skins, learn all about the life and eras of the formidable lizards and tick off a bunch of fun activities as they go. Once Gali was reassured they weren't real, he spent about fifteen minutes talking to some of the motion-triggered animatronic dinosaurs.

The kids loved these dinos, along with the crystal exhibit and various props and fossils. They even got to touch a real dinosaur bone, and a real meteorite too. Outside in the Dinosaur Garden, life-size fibreglass dinosaurs reminded us that it's a very good thing we don't live in the age of the

dinosaurs, as we probably wouldn't have lasted very long!

There are more kids' activities during summer holidays, including the opportunity to dig for fossils, and guided tours on the hour. Life-like replicas dominate the museum, which is small and manageable, and even has an outdoor play area, making it an ideal destination for families with younger kids.

The in and out passes also come in handy if you want to check out other attractions in Gold Creek, like Cockington Green Gardens across the road.

Dinosaurs ruled for hundreds of millions of years, until a ten to fifteen kilometre-wide asteroid struck the planet in what is now Mexico. The impact wiped the dinosaurs out in a massive extinction event, creating a chance opportunity for a tenacious little mammal to thrive.

Sixty-five million years of evolution later, your own tenacious little mammals can marvel at the legacy of these magnificent beasts, without the stress of being at the bottom of the food chain.

COCKINGTON GREEN GARDENS

Home for the gnomes

 Age minimum: None, kids younger than four years old enter free

 Open: Year round, closed Christmas Day and Boxing Day

 Visit: www.cockingtongreen.com.au

Conveniently located across the street from the National Dinosaur Museum is the family-run Cockington Green Gardens, an impressive labour of miniature-scale love that has been delighting kids for four decades.

The manicured Gardens are made up of two parts: the Original Display area and the International Area. The gardens are inspired by a family vacation to Torquay, England, in the 1970s, where founders Doug and Brenda Sarah fell in love with a little village called Cockington, nestled in dreamy English countryside.

Some people take photographs to remember their trips, but back in Australia, the Sarahs set about painstakingly recreating Cockington's street scenes, manors, cricket pitches, gardens, houses, people, cars and even soccer games (pay careful attention to some of the more unusual spectators).

Each model building is built at one-twelfth scale using durable fibreglass and aluminium, and there are some 1500 miniature people, animals and birds, all built by the Sarah family.

Up to 45,000 model bricks were laid for a single building! At first, the kids just wanted to run about and play with the figurines in what

Under a sunny sky, the blooming flowers and putting green grass fields added to the tranquillity of it all, making us wish we could magically transport ourselves to these bucolic English scenes.

We hopped on a miniature train, which gave us a much better idea of the sheer amount of work put into the two-acre gardens, and some stellar views of the second section, the International Area.

Refreshed with some tea from the Parsons Nose Garden Cafe, we strolled over to the International Area to visit the landmarks of thirty countries. High commissions and embassies were canvassed for feedback about which building

appeared to them to be a massive dollhouse. We had to hold them back and remind them that this was a place to look, but not touch.

to add into this miniature world, with financing from an Australian government tourism initiative.

There are amazing recreations depicting Petra (Jordan), Masada (Israel), Machu Picchu (Peru), the Red Fort (India), Stellenbosch (South Africa) and other famous landmarks from diverse countries like Ukraine, Mauritius, Colombia and Croatia. Some of the models were built overseas in the country they represent, and shipped in for display.

The kids pushed buttons to make miniature trains move and windmills spin, and my daughter managed to push her mother's buttons when, looking at a board listing all the flags of the countries represented, she declared that the most beautiful flag belongs to Argentina. Coming from the daughter of a Brazilian, this was like a scissor kick to the kidneys.

Once again, the attention to detail here was staggering, and the kids thoroughly enjoyed it all. Before the gardens closed, we made the most of the late afternoon sun, lazing on the smooth cut grass and watching the kids clamber all over model sheep and a non-miniature playground.

Unfortunately, life is not quite as idyllic or clear-cut as Cockingtown Gardens, but we can all pretend, at least for a little bit.

BE SMART WITH SCREENS

It's the time-honoured refrain: 'Dammit, Gertrude, these ~~wheels carts hula-hoops songs frisbees yo-yos radio series TV shows Shopkins~~ *screens* are going to ruin this generation! In *my* day, we kept ourselves busy with cow dung, silk worms and pieces of twig.'

First, the bad news: according to Australia's Department of Health, 'Evidence suggests that TV watched in the first two years of life may be connected with delays in language development'.

The department recommends that children younger than two years not spend *any* time, at all, watching TV or looking at a screen. Meanwhile, kids aged between two and five should have their screen time limited to less than one hour a day, which the American Academy of Paediatrics further adds should be 'high-quality programming' – whatever that is.

Now, before you start self-flagellating for being the world's worst parent, there is some good news:

➤ In an ideal world, your kids would be running free, learning by play every moment of the waking day, and be constantly stimulated and engaged with everything around them. There would also be no hunger, no corruption, no pollution, no incurable diseases, no crime and no ball tampering. As you may notice, we don't live in an ideal world, and it's very difficult to live by ideal guidelines.

➤ Most parents have every intention to limit screen time, but most parents also live in *reality*, where there's not always time to 'join in the play' and 'show kids how to run, jump and make big movements'. You're too busy cooking, clean-ing, packing, planning, driving, shopping and, in our case, travelling.

➤ You sure as hell watched more than an hour of TV a day, and look at you! You turned out okay (well, most of you, anyway).

. . . .

My neighbour in Canada has five kids under twelve. Her advice: 'As long as you love them unconditionally, they tend to figure their own shit out.' Human beings are nothing if not resilient.

Will watching seven hours of movies on a long-haul flight cause kids irreparable brain damage and lifelong social deficiencies? If they play educational apps at a restaurant while you eat, will it destroy their creativity? Or will the screen keep the kids busy long enough so you can get things done? And perhaps even sneak in a little bit of much-needed downtime.

Herein lies the problem with most recommendations for children's psychological wellbeing: they assume we live in an ideal world, and too rarely do they take into account the psychological wellbeing of *parents*.

If you don't get time to cook dinner, how are you supposed to feed the kids healthy, nutritious meals? If you don't get time to do the laundry and take out the rubbish and, dare I say it, sleep, how are you supposed to be patient, loving, caring and nurturing when your princess throws the bowl of porridge in your face because it isn't the exact consistency of three-day-old cement?

Yes, parents survived just fine before smartphones, tablets and their favourite shows on demand. Parents also survived just fine before cars, telephones and no-spill sippy cups. That doesn't mean those parents wouldn't have taken

advantage of our wondrous modern technology in a heartbeat. My Polish great-great-grandpa would have pulled out Peppa Pig on his iPad faster than you could say, 'My borscht is too runny'.

Remember, too, screen time when travelling is less consistent than screen time at home. Some days there's no time, want or need for any screen whatsoever. Actually, there are a lot of these days.

Some days, the kids will be binging like someone who's just discovered Episode 1, Season 1 of *Game of Thrones*. These days are often travel days.

Some days are normal: ABC Kids on a Saturday morning, or for a half-hour in the evening while you tidy up after dinner. Some days are all screen: when the kids are sick, grumpy and need couch time.

Despite the studies and Health Department recommendations, it's up to every parent to set their limits and use screens in a balanced way that makes sense for your situation.

Do remember though, if you pull that tablet or smartphone out at every opportunity, or have a TV constantly on, it will become just another toy, just more background noise, and you'll be stuck with books, toys *and* devices that won't do squat. Screens, especially the portable ones, are like espressos for kids, only they don't have to wire them up, they can also chill them out. Pace the usage, and it will work brilliantly for all concerned.

Rest assured that infrequent binge watching will likely be absorbed into your kid's resilient little systems along with infrequent binge eating of lollies on Halloween, and infrequent exposure to something graphic on the news. Kids get over it a lot quicker than parents get over the guilt.

CONTENT

Another factor not mentioned nearly enough in all these studies that highlight how bad a parent you are: the educational benefits of screens.

We live in an age where programming is smarter, and there are apps to engage every nuance of kids' curiosity.

When it comes to TV for young kids, stick with ABC Kids and refrain from tuning to commercial stations pumped full of manipulative and misleading advertising. As a rule, we found ABC Kids shows teach kids about new stuff, and positive messages and behaviours.

We found commercial family channels full of noise, colour, anger and merchandising. We don't have anything like ABC Kids in Canada, so take full advantage of it!

Handy tip

Want to stream a movie but worried it might have a single scene that will give your kid nightmares for months (and a lifelong phobia of lava monsters)? Common Sense Media (www.commonsensemedia.org) rates movies, TV shows and apps, and breaks them down into their themes and appropriateness for kids. It's a terrific guide and starting point to use your own discretion.

CHOOSING THE KIDS' NEXT FAVOURITE APP

Some apps are not cheap, but when you find the right app for the right age it can keep a kid busy for hours.

A simple Google search of 'best educational apps for X year olds' will come up with dozens of reviews. For our eighteen month old I see little difference between a flash card app and physical flash cards, other than the fact that he'll throw the physical cards all over the floor in about twelve seconds and I'll have to pick them up, again.

I guess it improves *my* hand-eye coordination. Beyond hand-eye coordination, building vocabulary and learning about colours, shapes and numbers, who's to say it's not training kids in the necessary digital literacy vital for the world they'll grow up in?

At least, thinking as much makes me feel a whole lot better.

Some of our favourite and more successful educational apps:

➤ ABC Kids Play
➤ Abby Monkey Basic Skills Pre K
➤ Busy Shapes
➤ Think & Learn Code-a-Pillar
➤ Duckie Deck Collection
➤ Drawing Desk
➤ Endless Reader
➤ Endless Alphabet
➤ Endless Numbers
➤ LetterSchool
➤ PBS Parents Play and Learn
➤ StoryBots
➤ Toca Nature

YOUTUBE AND YOUTUBE KIDS

First, don't let your kids watch YouTube. God knows what the hell the algorithm will auto-play after you watch a few Ozzy Man Reviews videos.

YouTube Kids limits what's on offer to kids, although it doesn't limit the unfortunate and mind-numbing trends of toy-unpacking, slime videos and el cheapo backroom productions. Our little one has a big thing for nursery rhyme videos.

Once Galileo starts, it's a deep, dark hole, as YouTube lines up infinite videos. Because I'd prefer the platform to focus on educational content, I've deleted YouTube Kids a couple of times only to find my kids somehow locate my main YouTube app buried in other folders. I've deleted YouTube off our tablet, and the kids still whine for it.

Music videos are fun to watch with the kids, provided you're monitoring the content (five year olds are not typically Ariana Grande's target audience). There's lots of advice about the benefits of watching videos with your kids, and pausing to discuss scenes and episodes. Of course, if you're watching videos with the kids, you might as well be playing with them in the first place.

TIPS FOR DEVICES

The judgement

Occasionally, you will be at a restaurant and receive sanctimonious glares from disapproving adults when your children are using a screen. If this happens, approach these people with a smile and ask them if they'd like to look after your kids while you

eat, because you're starving and the chicken nuggets you've inherited are getting cold.

They'll look down at their plates, and drop the glares instantly. If they agree, hooray, you've just scored yourself free sitters.

Make sure your kids have an extra large swig of concentrated apple juice before passing them over. The kids will also be thrilled you've taken away their screens and handed them to complete strangers.

The two-minute warning

It's a sound idea to always give your kids a two-minute warning before removing their device or turning off their screen. When they're on the device, they're locked in, fully engaged, and the outside world doesn't exist. Taking it away without some landing instructions tends to crash their overstimulated brains.

New apps

If you're introducing new apps, do it one at a time. Otherwise, it's like it's their birthday party: lots of new toys, lots of excitement, but they'll probably latch onto one and never give the others another look (at least until a sibling discovers the neglected toy/app, in which case, Princess won't be able to live without it).

The battery

Remember to charge your devices before heavy-lifting screen days, like flying or transit. There's nothing worse than a device with four per cent battery at the start of a six-hour flight.

The protective cases

Soft protective cases with handles and a screen protector are a must. Your kids *will* drop the screen, repeatedly, and likely spill milk, crackers and drool over it too. Often all at the same time.

The storage space

Every once in a while, look at your photos app to delete the hundreds of blurry and funny-face pictures your kid took when inadvertently stumbling upon the camera function.

You need the space for apps and movies. Netflix has a function that lets you download series and movies for offline viewing and it sure comes in handy – thanks, Netflix!

The double-check

Don't leave any hotel room or plane seat without checking you have all your devices, and that they haven't slipped under a couch or in the pouch of the seat in front of you.

People lose thousands of devices like this a year, but oddly enough, they rarely seem to turn up in the lost and found.

The headphones

Please don't be the parents who let their kids watch videos with the screen volume blaring in a restaurant. That's aggressively ruining other people's dining experiences, and your kids are already doing that as it is. Invest in a pair of headphones for the kids, please and thank you.

KEEP A TRAVEL BLOG

Keep an oldschool scrapbook, or upload photos and memories to a blog as you go. Not only can you save and print this material for lifelong safekeeping, but you can also share your experiences with friends and family as you go.

We created an online trip log for our journey to reflect with the kids on each day just passed, and to prepare for the day to come. We captured what we learned (as parents and kids), the best part, the worst part, what we did, where we ate and the people we met.

It has since become a wonderful document of our journey, although sticking with it every day turned out to be a lot more work than we anticipated. Check out www.esrockingkids. com to follow our daily adventures.

QUEENSLAND

EAT STREET NORTHSHORE

Kids and dogs welcome

 Age minimum: None

 Open: Year round

 Visit: www.eatstreetmarkets.com

Young kids are picky eaters and rarely sit still. No matter how expensive the dining establishment or how positive your intentions, countless meals in restaurants become masterclasses in patience – and the redistribution of food from table to floor.

If only all dining out experiences were as fun and fruitful as Brisbane's Eat Street. Operating every weekend all year, it's the very definition of good food and fun for the whole family. The space itself is unique: 180 shipping containers on the northern bank of the Brisbane River arranged into small kitchens, bars, stores and stages.

It's a self-contained neighbourhood with surprises around every corner, including three live music stages, performance artists and themed alleys. Picture neon lights, an open-sky theatre, art installations, boutique stores and an entire laneway full of decadent treats.

The meals on offer are a cut above, but are deliberately priced under $15, with something for every taste. Unlike the dross served in shopping centre food courts, the diversity of international cuisines is matched by the passion of the chefs, hailing from Hungary, Peru, China, Turkey, Brazil, Greece or Queensland itself.

Although there's plenty of

seating, it does get busy, so you'll want to park at a long wooden bench, meet some neighbours and sample different courses from

different takeaway containers. With my kids wired up – courtesy of cheeky visits to the Swedish Candy Bay, which looks like a blue-lit Scandinavian pharmacy, and Professor Fairy Floss, which looks like the sugary workshop of a madman – we danced with the tweens at the main stage, entertained by a great cover band and dance troop.

It's a wonderfully festive atmosphere, the kind you typically have to work very hard to find. Raquel pleaded to get her henna tattoo, illuminated by an LED flower headdress that made her easy to find as the place filled up with families,

couples, tourists and even pets.

Eat Street organisers told me they're passionate about bringing great, affordable food and fun to everyone, including their dogs.

There's a small entrance fee, ample parking and enough variety to ensure everyone can eat whatever it is they want. Eat Street is an institution for locals, and a must for families visiting Brisbane. If only all holiday meals were this easy.

JUNGLE SURFING

Aaaaa-aaa-aaa-aaa

 Age minimum: Three years. Not every five year old will love it like mine did, and be aware there's no turning back

 Open: Year round

 Visit: www.junglesurfing.com.au

Intergenerational travel is becoming more and more popular, for as rewarding as it is to travel with kids, having grandparents along makes for even richer memories (and more importantly, someone to watch the kids while you sneak away for a cheeky date with your partner).

Even if you don't have a great relationship with your parents, travel creates a different space, one that tends to chill everyone out and ensure good times ahead. If your folks happen to be visiting from Canada, and together you find yourselves in Tropical North Queensland, all the better.

I cast my net wide for an adventure fit for ages five to seventy-two, which is how my daughter, my father and I ended up hanging from a metal wire high in the canopy of the world's oldest rainforest.

It was a gorgeous drive from our hotel in Port Douglas to the UNESCO-protected Daintree Rainforest, where we ferried over croc-infested waters into a landscape that looked positively Jurassic.

We entered tunnels of palms, figs and ferns the likes of which you won't find anywhere else in the world. A sign for the Daintree Ice Cream Co. demanded a hard brake, followed shortly by some of the most delicious and unique ice-cream in the country. Davidson

plum, sugar banana and wattle seed anyone?

Our destination was Cape Tribulation where a company called Jungle Surfing has hitched up seven ziplines in a UNESCO World Heritage site. I call that a feat of both engineering and expert red-tape cutting.

Kitted out in harnesses and helmets, we said g'day to a massive golden orb weaver spider, and walked through the jungle to an unusual human hamster wheel that elevated us to the first tree platform. Another great feat of local engineering! One zipline in, Raquel officially declared it the best day ever.

'Faster! Is that one longer? I want to go by myself! I want to hang upside down – no wait, I don't want to hang upside down!' So small and so light, Raquel practically floated between the trees with a watermelon-sized smile the entire time – not a whine, moan or meltdown in sight.

So well behaved was she that I wish I could install ziplines in the living room. My dad, meanwhile, enjoyed flying through the trees without having to hike among creatures he'd rather not think about, and I simply enjoyed all three of us spending quality time together. In essence, this is the joy of travelling with multiple generations.

As my daughter conquered each platform like an explorer braving new planets, I asked the folks at Jungle Surfing how kids typically do on their ziplines, which are offered to children as young as three years old. They told me that much of it has to do with the attitude of the parents. If the parents are nervous and neurotic, the kids pick up on it, and they become whiny and scared.

Young kids are a blank slate. Most don't know what they should be afraid of, or why. Ziplining is one of the safer adventures a family can do, and yet our guide shared stories of young kids crying because their parent was freaking out about the height (although why anyone would look down instead of at the incredible forest surrounding them is beyond me).

Some kids have antennae that amplify the emotions of their parents, so I suggest braving a smile, even if you are terrified.

As for the older participants, ziplining is not too physically demanding, as gravity does all the work. Jungle Surfing in the Daintree is an ideal adventure in a unique location, which proved a cross-generational hit for our delighted family of travellers.

WILDLIFE HABITAT

Where the wild things are

 Age Minimum: None. Kids younger than four years old enter free

 Open: Year round, closed Christmas Day

 Visit: www.wildlifehabitat.com.au

Set against the backdrop of the world's oldest rainforest, Tropical North Queensland is full of life and colour. You can start your day early with Breakfast with the Birds, which has been a regional highlight for more than two decades at the Wildlife Habitat, a popular bird and wildlife sanctuary in Port Douglas.

After a tropical buffet breakfast to the soundtrack of the chirps of seventy-five different bird species, we met the zookeeper and superhero mum of five, Bec, who asked Raquel what her favourite experience of our journey had been so far. Without dropping a beat, Raquel replied: 'Well, let's see how

fun this morning is, and then I'll tell you'. Cheeky bugger.

With passion and enthusiasm, Bec showed us around the woodland, wetland, savannah and rainforest sections of the habitat, where we quickly spotted our first tree kangaroo. Wildlife Habitat is one of only two parks in the country where you can see the rare Lumholtz's tree kangaroo, which sports mask-like colouring that makes it look like a bandit scoping a bank.

With roo feed in hand, we met eastern grey kangaroos, agile, swamp and northern nail-tail wallabies and lots of ducks and emus. We saw a crocodile waiting

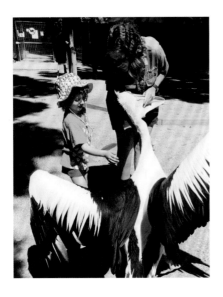

to pounce on a bird that would likely regret its decision to land in a saltie's enclosure, while some pushy magpie geese snuck up and plucked feed right out of our hands.

We learned about the spotted quoll, Australia's apex marsupial carnivore, and popped into the reptile section to see some active snakes slithering rhythmically. Having already driven up to Cape Tribulation, we finally saw our first cassowary (outside a road warning sign).

With its bright colours and distinctive helmet, called a casque, I figured it was best not to mention that cassowaries are, along with ostriches, the only birds definitely known to have killed humans. Blame their dagger-sharp claws and territorial nature.

Of course, the kids demanded

koala action, and they're always as cute, soft and cuddly as they look in the pictures. Koalas also smell like eucalyptus, proving perhaps that you are what you eat. (By the way, did you know it's only legal to hold and snuggle a koala in Queensland, Western Australia and South Australia?)

During the North Queensland Reptile Experience, we got to hang out with a large, friendly black-headed python, and learned it would shed skin three times its body length. We discovered frog-mouth owls and all sorts of other creatures but, most importantly, we learned from Bec that it's possible to be a mother of five kids and hundreds of birds and animals at the same time.

My wife reminded me that we are parents to a unique set of animals too, prone to attack us with meltdowns, but also heart-melting cuddles and hilarious and surprising observations. At the end of the day, Raquel told Bec she'd had her Best. Day. Ever.

Without having to worry about money, logistics, cooking, packing, driving, emails and other five year olds waking her up fifteen times at night, what little girl wouldn't have the Best. Day. Ever. with so many wild and beautiful Australian creatures?

MACKAY

Family travel purgatory

 Age minimum: None

 Open: Year round

 Visit: www.mackayregion.com

For the most part, logistics on our journey across Australia ran remarkably smoothly. A few rough edges, sure, but given the pace and the fact that we'd be visiting about fifty destinations in just six months, things tended to line up well.

Eventually, we were bound to hit an unavoidable scheduling snag. Like, say, departing Mackay, Queensland, for Darwin, Northern Territory. Although the distance isn't that great, limited transport options meant two full days of travel, a late checkout and then ten hours to do . . . something in Mackay, until our evening flight to Brisbane.

We'd overnight at Brisbane Airport, and then have ten hours to do . . . something there, too, until our flight to Darwin would finally touch down after midnight. Mackay is a mining town, a pass-through town and a town you could maybe spend a couple days exploring – unless it's raining cats and hamsters. In which case, there's no taking kids to the Bluewater Lagoon waterpark, or driving to a local beach.

Instead, we walked to the public library, which is a great place to take young kids anywhere, anytime. We read a zillion books, played with arts and crafts, had an excellent

lunch nearby and returned to the library to do it all over again. The librarians must have thought we were squatters.

The library closed at 6pm, so we still had four hours to go, with Gali skipping his nap and acting like a punch-drunk big-horned sheep, head banging his way forward, falling over his feet.

While I had the kids in the library, Ana snuck off to cut her hair pixie short. Her long hair was driving her crazy, and now she would have a lot less of it. It also killed ninety minutes, which is probably more important in the context of the day.

Ana had committed to the cut before realising the hairdresser was eighteen years old and didn't exactly know how to cut hair. But ninety minutes away from the kids is ninety minutes away from the kids, however you cut it.

We looked to the local cinemas to see if we could kill a couple of hours, but there was nothing appropriate for toddlers. And so, as the parrots kicked up a sunset ruckus and bats flew overhead, we walked to the city's most popular attraction, Caneland Central shopping centre.

In Mackay, the shops close at 4pm, inexplicably early (for us city

folks anyway), and so we wandered about the deserted centre like lost souls in a retail ghost town.

We were, literally, the only people in the place, and it's not small. For some reason, the shopping centre was still blasting terrible 90s pop music, perhaps because they knew nobody would be there to listen to it. As Raquel got to bust dance moves to Ace of Base, my wife strongly insisted that, after our day of family travel purgatory, all she wanted was definitely and unequivocally *not* another baby.

We lounged on public coin-operated massage chairs, trying not to think about how many people had lounged on the same public coin-operated massage chairs before us, and whether they were sweating when they did.

Eventually a South African taxi driver named Cecil got us to Mackay Airport, telling us it's a great city to live in, although admittedly there's not much to actually do in Mackay, especially in low season during stormy weather.

You'd think that days devoid of exciting activities would be instantly forgettable. And yet the absurdity of killing time in a deserted shopping centre, getting a dramatic haircut out of sheer boredom and spending slow hours in a library somehow made it entirely memorable.

After so much go-go-go, we caught our breaths with a rare opportunity to appreciate how much we got right when planning our journey. Every day on the road is a blessing, even if it takes a while to discover what that blessing is.

CAPE HILLSBOROUGH

Roos for sunrise

 Age minimum: None

 Open: Year round

 Visit: www.capehillsboroughresort.com.au

Getting up in the very early hours of the morning is often difficult for me, especially when the kids have woken me up four times in the middle of the night because it was too dark, too hot, too light and too cold.

I often want to hit snooze on my alarm clock, and I want to hit snooze on life. Still, I know the best experiences make you want to bounce out of bed no matter what time it is, because you know it's going to be special.

This was the case at 5am one morning in Mackay. Despite my daughter's late-night antics, I was relieved to see her sharing my enthusiasm. Together we hopped in the car and drove forty minutes north on a winding road to Cape Hillsborough Nature Tourist Park, just in time for one of the most epic sunrises in the country.

About a decade ago, kangaroos and wallabies started to show up on the beach shortly before the egg-yolk sun broke on the horizon. The tourist park's owners would feed them, and about a dozen guests would get up early to share this quintessential Australian coastal sunrise. Word quickly got out, Qantas featured the experience in an in-flight safety video, travel writers like me showed up and next thing you knew, hundreds of people were gathering on the beach each morning.

All well and good, but not everyone has the good sense to keep their distance and refrain from feeding sugary crap to the increasingly emboldened animals. Kangaroos have been known to attack overzealous and idiotic tourists, as well they should.

This is why authorities recently decided it best to regulate the Cape Hillsborough sunrise experience, charging a fee for live commentary from a guide about the region's history and wildlife conservation.

I parked the car and my daughter and I walked along the gorgeous beach towards a crowd of people gathered up ahead. The animals were already there, and the sun was just about to make its splash.

International tourists were obviously more taken with the sight of kangaroos and wallabies, but regardless of your experience with marsupials, it makes for a very special wildlife encounter, in a very special place and at a very special time.

Memory cards were put to work as cameras big and small did their best to capture the moment. Sunrises are a golden hour for photography, but we rarely take advantage because it's also too damn early. Clear, orange light at sunrise makes for beautiful shots.

It's all over in about five to ten minutes. The animals scatter to the bush, and the people towards their cars or, more conveniently, breakfast in their cabins, huts or motorhomes inside the nature park. Either way, it's a sunrise kids of all ages won't mind getting up for.

WHITEHAVEN BEACH

Squeaky sands

 Age minimum: None

 Open: Year round

 Visit: www.cruisewhitsundays.com

Seventy-four islands make up the archipelago known as the Whitsundays, with ninety-six per cent of the 30,000-hectare area protected as part of the Great Barrier Reef ecosystem.

The reef here is faring better than the reef up north around Cairns, which has been devastated by climate change and tourism. Whether you base yourself in the mainland centre of Airlie Beach, or further into the Whitsundays on Hamilton Island or Daydream Island, this is a stunningly beautiful part of the world, and Whitehaven Beach is renowned as the most stunning part of that stunning part.

We signed up for a half-day trip to this legendary beach, located on the east coast of Whitsunday Island (not to be confused with the archipelago itself). Driving in that morning from Townsville, we had a slight mishap involving an oral explosion of porridge, courtesy of Galileo.

We thought we'd become pretty good at recognising his pre-puke signs, but, obviously, not that good. Not for the first time, we were saved by buffering our arrival time and departing early, just in case.

We caught our boat at the Cruise Whitsundays terminal, and had to endure some unusually rough seas

that morning. This is why the family travel pros carry two extra changes of clothes, and plastic bags for puke-infused discards.

After dropping off and picking up passengers at Hamilton Island, the large, modern catamaran continued onward to Whitehaven Bay, where the protected waters were now as calm as a turquoise mirror.

Having transferred to a smaller boat for a beach landing, we found ourselves on seven kilometres of paradise. Fine ninety-eight per cent quartz sand squeaked with every step, the crystal-clear sea lapped the beach like a kitten's tongue to milk, and a deep blue sky warmed us overhead.

Friendly Cruise Whitsundays staff put out toys, umbrellas, shade tents and an activity board, with fish feeding, beach cricket, a sand castle competition and volleyball all on the agenda. Some day trippers were content to walk along the crescent-shaped beach, keeping an eye out for white-bellied sea eagles, iguanas and monitor lizards.

Gali passed out in the shade of a tent, as his mother polished her rings with the sand. The quartz does a splendid job restoring shine to wedding rings, and the Whitsundays do a splendid job of restoring shine to marriages, too.

Having fed dart fish swimming between her legs and clobbered her first beach cricket ball, Raquel had a blast doing what kids do on beaches everywhere, thanks to the spades and shovels provided.

Stinger suits are also provided, as the region is cursed by box and Irukandji jellyfish. Their stings might be rare as a unicorn, but still, you don't want to be stung by a unicorn, especially on holiday.

Along with tours to Hamilton Island and its outer-reef pontoon, Cruise Whitsundays offers morning and afternoon half-day tours to Whitehaven Beach, which benefits from the sunset cruise back to Airlie Beach, best enjoyed on the outer deck, where you'll be comforted by a warm ocean breeze, and a colourful sky you'll never forget.

FRASER ISLAND

Doing it the way you can

 Age minimum: None

 Open: Year round

 Visit: www.whalesong.com.au

When you travel with young kids, every once in a while you're going to have to accept that there are certain places and activities that, well, are just not made for little ones.

Some parents won't have any issues whatsoever schlepping their kids on challenging adventures, and who are we to judge? Personally, as much as I wanted to spend a week camping on Fraser Island, the thought of doing it with two kids too young to appreciate the effort involved made no sense to me.

With so much to see along Queensland's coast, instead I hoped to find a manageable full-day excursion that would still deliver some of the wonder of the world's largest sand island, but with more manageable logistics and, dare I say it, time to actually enjoy it.

The friendly folks at the Hervey Bay Discovery Park believed Whalesong Cruises would tick all these boxes, provided we could pull my daughter away from her new-found buddies at the jumping pillow.

Fraser Island is 1840 square kilometres of coastal dunes, rainforest, pristine beaches and crystal-clear, quartz-filtered lakes. There are

no roads on the island, and the only way to explore it is with an all-wheel drive, or by boat. The MV *Whalesong 2* has three extra-wide decks for marine wildlife viewing, a comfortable interior, and enthusiastic staff dedicated to memorable family excursions.

The skipper let our kids on the bridge to pretend they were piloting the sixteen-metre vessel, and all was well. We crossed the shallow channel between the mainland and Fraser Island in a light drizzle, and arrived an hour later at Coongul Creek on the island's west coast, a remote area removed from the all-wheel drive traffic.

Parked on the beach, out came the sea kayaks and fishing rods, and the sun too. No sooner had Raquel cast her first ever line than she snagged her first ever fish, resulting in the sudden realisation that the fish we eat are actually fish in the sea. We released her tiny little catch to the waves, which pleased her to no end.

Of course we were hoping to catch sight of the world's most purebred dingoes, a draw for many visitors to the island, but the dingoes remained scarce. This is a wise survival tactic, given the cull that took place as a result of a tragic attack on the island many years ago. Some dingoes on Fraser Island did, in fact, take someone's baby, when they killed a nine-year-old boy in 2001. One more reason to keep our eyes on the kids

as we soaked in the tea-coloured creek next to the beach.

Upon learning about rare dingo attacks and the half-dozen people evacuated earlier that summer for box jellyfish stings, Ana was more than content to keep our visit short,

easy and sweet, and we returned to Hervey Bay later that afternoon.

Sure, we didn't do the full Fraser Island experience of exploring Lake McKenzie, Central Station, the wreck of the SS *Maheno* and the green waters of Lake Wabby. It would have been great, but with young kids in tow, we felt it was more important for our sanity to do what we could, when and how we could best do it. Sound family travel advice I wish we'd known from the start.

Besides, it always leaves something for next time, when the kids are potty-trained, open to camping, and able to appreciate the unique landscape, wildlife and history of somewhere as remarkable as Fraser Island.

SOUTH BANK PARKLANDS

A world-class play

 Age minimum: None

 Open: Year round

 Visit: www.visitbrisbane.com.au/south-bank?sc_lang=en-au

When it comes to entertaining young kids, I have to give it to Brisbane. With its wide, pedestrian-only streets, fifty-two-hectare Botanic Gardens, Children's Art Centre at QAGOMA and scenic riverbank walks, there was a lot to do from our hotel base in the CBD.

Just across the bridge was the South Bank Parklands, which became our favourite urban hangout in the entire country. It consists of a number of excellent playgrounds for kids of different ages, chock full of swings, bridges, climbing walls and slides.

To help with the tropical weather, there's the man-made Streets Beach, with its white sands overlooking a swimming lagoon, and plenty of spots to picnic under the palm trees. Aquativity is a huge water play area, with fountains, tipping buckets, spray features and a large, shallow play area for the little ones. It also has plenty of shaded seating, barbecue areas and easy access to toilets and showers. The larger Boat Pool is a more traditional public swimming pool.

We loved that all of these kid-friendly destinations are available free of charge every day of the year, drawing manageable crowds of locals and tourists. There are plenty of cafes and restaurants nearby too, as well as market stalls and food trucks.

Raquel celebrated her fifth birthday in Brisbane, and we gave her the choice of what she wanted to do, and where she wanted to go.

Her answer: dress up like Emma Wiggle, go to the big playground by the river, get a piñata and eat the twisty potato on a stick. We were happy to oblige for our hardened little road warrior, of course!

With all the kids about, and with the help of the piñata's sugary insides, Raquel made quick friends.

Later, we explored the pathways covered with flowers, an interactive art installation and the less popular Picnic Island Green, shaded by a giant fig tree. South Bank also runs a free program called Kids Collective every week for under-fives, no registration required.

It takes a healthy chunk of municipal vision to recognise that families need a place to park

themselves, whether they're travelling or not. That Brisbane created this space overlooking the river and city, in such close proximity to the CBD, is one of the reasons it doesn't need to market itself as Australia's *next* world city. It already is.

RAINFORESTATION NATURE PARK

All in one

 Age minimum: None

 Open: Year round, closed Christmas Day

 Visit: www.rainforest.com.au

'Okay kids, today we'll explore the rainforest of Tropical Northern Queensland on board an amphibious World War II Army Duck. Then we'll meet some local Indigenous fellas who'll teach us how to a) throw a spear, b) throw a boomerang, c) blow the didgeridoo and d) do a traditional dance.

'We'll eat some delicious kebabs and then feed some kangaroos, visit some devils, cassowaries, wombats, pythons and koalas, and peer into the enclosure of some monster crocodiles. Incredibly, we will do all of this in one place, and if you can refrain from puking on the winding mountain road to get there, you might even leave the gift shop with a new stuffed toy. What do you say?'

Rainforestation Nature Park is an immersive, one-stop exploration of Queensland culture and Australiana, popular with international tour buses and, given the amount you can do in the one place, popular with parents who don't want to visit six different attractions.

We kicked things off at the Pamagirri Aboriginal Experience, where welcoming Indigenous guides introduced us to their local culture, regaled in full body paint. At a boomerang demonstration, we quickly discovered we'd have more luck throwing pianos at the birds, but the kids relished the opportunity to throw stuff as hard as they liked and not get in trouble.

Our Pamagirri guide, Shaun, played the didgeridoo like we've never heard it before, and taught us about the instrument: how the shorter the didgeridoo is, the higher the pitch, and that didgeridoo isn't even the correct Indigenous name for the instrument. It actually goes by many different names, the most common being *yidi yidi*.

Next, he used a sort of wooden slingshot to increase the speed and force of a spear throw, amazing us all with how far his spear travelled into an adjacent field. A dance performance followed in a seated amphitheatre, a cultural experience ideal for time-conscious tour buses, and parents on guard for meltdowns.

Here, we learned how songs and dance were used for millennia to pass on knowledge. Once again, Raquel couldn't resist the opportunity to hop on stage and do her skinny-leg shimmy.

The activities are carefully timed so you can leave one and move right onto the next. In our case, we headed off to board the Army Duck Tour. The affable Duck Captain Murray clearly loves his job, pointing out basket plants and wild sweet potatoes, rare orchids, stinging trees, tropical fruit and some of the other 900 species of trees on the property. The camouflaged Army Duck ground up and down steep terrain before elegantly gliding into a large pond and showcasing its amphibiousness.

Wildlife Park. There, a fearsome five-metre croc has a reputation for killing a dozen of his former girl-friends, and is appropriately called Jack the Ripper.

More benign are the koala and lazing kangaroos, and any activity that ends with animals is going to be a hit with the kids.

Rainforestation is a slick nature park owned by a company that runs other attractions in the region, and the kids certainly won't notice or mind the mass-tourism aspect of it. As for the stuffed toy, it would have been useful to plug Gali's mouth, as he once again demonstrated his uncanny ability to puke on every winding road in Queensland.

We spotted eastern water dragons basking in the sun, and emerged onto the dirt track for the forty-five-minute round trip back to the base.

There are three quick and easy buffet restaurants on site, and it's a short walk over to the Koala and

Shortly thereafter, the day's non-stop activity ensured both kids passed out sound asleep on the drive home to Port Douglas.

HUDSONS CIRCUS

Under the tent

 Age minimum: None

 Open: Year round

 Visit: www.hudsoncircus.com

I have vivid and deeply fond memories of my grandfather taking me to the circus. Granted, it was back in the days when people smoked on planes, never wore seatbelts and believed there was nothing wrong with training elephants and lions for their entertainment.

The big top has certainly fallen out of favour, while the world's most popular circus, Cirque du Soleil, has dispensed with grit and popcorn in favour of hugely elaborate sets and exorbitant ticket prices, elevating the experience far beyond the reach of most two year olds.

I've seen about a dozen Cirque shows over the years, and found them to be slick productions with jaw-dropping acrobatic performances, mostly devoid of soul.

As we drove into Mackay, we saw posters advertising Hudsons Circus, the largest travelling circus in Australia. Immediately, I wondered if some of that old-school circus magic would touch my kids. Hay underfoot, the derring-do of the trapeze, giggles at the clown, the reverb of the ringmaster.

Given the costs, logistics and lifestyle, running a modern circus must be a high-wire act. With kids accustomed to Pixar and Netflix, and lion acts a thing of the past, how did Hudsons Circus fare? Brilliantly.

From the first acrobatic

performance to the ponies, the loud motorbikes spiralling inside the Cage of Death to the trapeze, both my kids were absolutely spellbound. We quickly realised that the popcorn seller was also the trapeze artist, and he was also the motorbike guy and the acrobat. In a family-run circus, everyone performs multiple roles, and I have no doubt they take down and set up the tent too.

Goldie the Clown had the kids in stitches, and the sight of camels and water buffalos doing tricks around the ring kept them rapt. These animals, it should be noted, were rescued from meat factories.

The tricks were not always successful, but we applauded the brave effort, and enjoyed meeting the performers during the break, and sitting under the big yellow tent for the kind of entertainment you don't see much of these days.

Raquel even participated in one of the acts, along with a dozen other kids pulled from the matinee's audience. Hudsons Circus isn't too pricey, and the fact that it's small and somewhat frayed at the edges creates an enduring charm.

No matter where you might be, if the kids need some fun and the circus is in town, grab some popcorn, take your seat, and enjoy a clown trip down memory lane.

STAYING HEALTHY

THE SUN

Despite my best efforts, I could not find any proof whatsoever to back up the claim that there is a hole in the ozone layer above Australia. Australians suffer from high rates of skin cancer because the majority of Australians have the wrong skin type for this environment and enjoy an outdoorsy beach culture. Lacking melanin is perfectly dandy if you live in Europe, but it's like bringing a knife to a gunfight in the Australian heat.

Moral of the story: ozone hole or no, be sun smart and make sure both kids and parents are protected.

Did you know that oxybenzone, one of the key ingredients in sunscreen, has been shown to reduce sperm count in men and increase infertility in women? Some frustrated parents might wish to apply sunscreen, even if it's raining outside.

In Canada, we make a big deal of using zinc-based natural sunscreens, because we're not into hormone disruptors, and we never see any sun. We would have loved to use more nature-based sunscreen products in Australia, but found they weren't readily as available, or as affordable, as we would have hoped.

DON'T PANIC

Kids hurt themselves. Usually they get over it in a recovery time to rival Deadpool's, but occasionally they don't. Don't panic. It's the first thing they teach you in a first-aid course: calmness leads to better decision-making.Clean up the blood, assess the injury and get to a hospital if you need to.

Fevers, tummy aches, diarrhoea, constipation – your kids are susceptible to all of it, but serious cases are rare. Carry a simple first-aid kit (with bandaids, disinfectant, infant-safe painkillers, Travacalm, after sun lotion and bite spray).

Our kids have been vaccinated, because we prefer a world without measles, diphtheria, mumps and chicken pox. In Australia, we didn't feel the need to get typhoid shots, despite the pushy sales job at our local travel clinic.

WASHING HANDS

Perhaps the best health habit to pass onto your kids is hand-washing – a habit many kids are hesitant to adopt.

Perhaps they hate washing their hands because they know just how much we want them to do it, especially after playing in a shopping centre playground. We don't want to turn our kids into paranoid germaphobes, but they need to understand why licking their fingers like lollypops after crawling on an airport floor is not a great idea.

We used hand sanitiser warily, because in 2016, the US Food and Drug Administration banned nineteen ingredients found in antibacterial products. Washing hands with soap and water is best, particularly before meals.

When you have kids who fist each other's mouths for the sheer joy of it, you just do the best you can.

INSECTS AND FLIES

Toddlers and infants are too young for the safe and repetitive use of DEET (N,N-Diethyl-meta-toluamide), which is found in common insect repellents.

Fortunately, there are natural products with citronella, lemongrass and eucalyptus, but they are harder to find and a lot more expensive. When we got to Thailand and Bali, mosquitoes the size of swallows seemed to enjoy the taste of our natural repellents. Gali's arms and legs were feasted on, and of course he picked the bites and scabs. We eventually started burning those little blue mats, figuring whatever they release into the air to kill the mosquitoes is better than the carnage on his legs and hands.

Your best defence against mozzies is to cover up with loose clothing, and avoid being outside at dusk and dawn. As for what I call the Australian sticky fly – the insect that simply must find shade in the cool of your ears, mouth and nostrils – there's not much you can do but teach your kids the bush wave.

Handy tip
When checking into hotel rooms with infants and young children, remove any decorative items that the kids will want to play with and destroy (trays, vases, statues).

Make them aware of any steps or sharp corners, and feel free to rearrange the furniture to keep them away from edges, bookcases, standing lamps and windows that are not kid-safe. The hotel might not be thrilled with the rearrangement, but safety comes first.

TOILETS AND NAPPIES

We travelled with one potty-trained kid, and one kid in nappies. Both presented challenges.

When my potty-trained daughter needs to go, it's usually at that point when she needs to *go now*! This led to some interesting experiences on the side of highways and trails, in shopping centres and busy streets.

I will say this: Australia has some of the cleanest and best-maintained public toilets on the planet. We did not have to contend with anything like The Worst Toilet in Scotland (see the film *Trainspotting*), an ordeal I've faced in many other countries.

As a dad, it's never fun taking a little girl into the men's latrines (see the MCG section p 35) but little girls have tricks, too.

While the toilets themselves are generally in good shape, Australia does not have enough nappy change tables in their public toilets. Our nappy changes took place whenever and wherever needed.

My wife quickly became a pro at the standing nappy change, or changing a number two in the back seat of the car, where precision is key.

We always carry little plastic bags, like the kind used to clean up after dogs, to dispose of nappies with number twos without mess (although, regrettably, not without stench).

TRAVEL INSURANCE

Our year abroad was mostly a healthy one. We ate well, exercised frequently, spent a lot of time outdoors and kept ourselves busy doing interesting things.

There were some minor issues – tummy aches, sniffles, bruises, skinned knees and mosquito bites – but never anything serious.

Still, travel insurance is a must. On this trip, we only used our policy once – not even in Australia – when a balloon popped and cut my wife's retina in Thailand. She received first-class treatment in Chiang Mai and later in Bangkok, all covered by insurance.

The peace of mind alone is worth it, and yes, accidents do happen. Make sure your policy covers the entire family before setting out on your big adventure.

NORTHERN
TERRITORY

CROCOSAURUS COVE

In a while, crocodile

 Age minimum: None (fifteen years for the Cage of Death)

 Open: Year round, closed Christmas Day

 Visit: www.crocosauruscove.com

'They'll snatch you right off the beach!' said our taxi driver in Darwin, fortunately referring to the crocodiles, not overfriendly locals walking down Smith Street. Crocodylus porosus, aka the estuarine crocodile, aka the saltwater crocodile, is the world's largest living reptile, and it sits top of mind in the Top End.

Prowling the shores and watering holes in the wet season, each year some idiot ignores all the warning signs and becomes lunch for a saltie, although this is the kind of information you don't really want to be sharing with the kids, especially when you invite them to slip into a wading pool to get a better view of the baby crocs.

Kids older than fifteen can even take on the Cage of Death to be lowered into a pool with some terrifyingly large adult crocs. All this and more is on offer at Crocosaurus Cove, a wildlife attraction located in the heart of Darwin's CBD. Kids and crocs don't feel like a natural fit, but kids and animals of any description go hand in . . . spiky foot.

In the pools are some of the largest, most belligerent and aggressive crocs in the region, removed from watering holes after chewing outboard motors and not playing nice with others at crocodile farms.

Daily demonstrations, covered in the ticket price, include the Big Croc Feeding Show (handlers use a

very long stick) and an opportunity for the kids to feed baby crocs in a smaller enclosure (with a much shorter stick).

Watching a 700-kilogram legend like Burt, the same croc who starred in *Crocodile Dundee*, launch himself into the air to grab a piece of meat leaves little doubt that wrestling a croc into submission would be like stopping a moving bullet train.

A handy machine demonstrates that crocs have the mightiest bite of any animal, equivalent to dropping a three-ton brick on your foot and ten times more powerful than the bite of a great white. Hearing the *whump* of the machine, and later Burt's impressive jaws, sent my

daughter jumping into my arms.

Crocodiles may be many things, but unlike our visits to other animal parks, not once did I hear the word 'cute'. The family-friendly wading pool looked more impressive than it was, in that the glass and water were pretty murky so we couldn't see the baby crocs very clearly.

The same can't be said for the Cage of Death, which gets you closer to a crocodile than you'd ever want to be. Parents of young kids might argue that any long road trip with little ones in the car is also a Cage of Death, but at least the car windows aren't scratched up by a crocodile attempting to get inside and extract your tasty innards.

For younger kids, the adjacent

Reptile House has the largest display of Aussie reptiles in the country, with three shows daily for guests to learn more about the resident snakes and lizards.

You'll also find a World of Crocs exhibition with plenty of fascinating info and wax models to help distinguish your saltie from your alligator. Professional onsite photographers captured the kids holding a baby croc with a wrapped snout and unusually calm demeanour.

Crocs this little might even make great pets, if it weren't for the whole growing up and eating people thing. Plan to spend about three hours here pre- or post-lunch, with the various shows conveniently scheduled around midday.

Exit through the gift shop with newfound respect for this magnificent and terrifying prehistoric creature, and good luck convincing anyone to join you for a walk on the beach afterwards.

MUSEUM AND ART GALLERY OF THE NORTHERN TERRITORY

The top museum in the Top End

 Age minimum: Kids younger than sixteen years old must be accompanied by an adult

Open: Year round, closed Christmas Day, Boxing Day, New Year's Day and Good Friday

Visit: www.magnt.net.au

The Museum and Art Gallery of the Northern Territory (MAGNT) might not have the big-budget modern sheen of other museums around the country, but for young kids, this must-visit Darwin attraction has plenty going for it.

For starters, it's a lot more manageable than some big-name museums, meaning you can actually see and do everything in a two- to three-hour visit without being overwhelmed, with plenty of time to discuss the exhibits and participate in activities.

It also has super friendly staff, and a Discovery Centre that kept my daughter completely engaged with microscopes, pop art and button making.

The MAGNT has a natural history section, with taxidermies of the region's creatures, along with skeletons and skins and other stuff that toes the line between fascinating and creepy. One of the highlight exhibits is a five-metre-long stuffed croc, affectionately known as Sweetheart. This 780-kilogram monster had a taste for boats in a local billabong. A botched relocation in the 1970s led to Sweetheart's demise and immaculate restoration as a

conversation piece, his jaws opened wide enough to accommodate an overcurious toddler.

Further along is a fascinating exhibit about Cyclone Tracy, the devastating storm that flattened Darwin on Christmas Day 1974. The most compact storm ever recorded in history resulted in dozens of deaths, destruction of eighty per cent of the city's housing and the

evacuation of thirty thousand people.

The exhibit sparked an interesting discussion with my daughter about the powerful forces of nature, given she'll be growing up in a world where extreme weather events will be a regular occurrence. With a warning that some visitors might find the experience upsetting, a small room plays a recording of what the cyclone sounded like as it blasted through Darwin.

Whether it was the dark space or noise, it was enough to spook Raquel and send us in search of sunnier exhibits. Indigenous art and a visiting exhibition from a famous modern artist easily fit the bill.

At the MAGNT, entrance fee is by donation, making it a particularly affordable family outing in Darwin, and the facility is pram-friendly. The main museum is located at Bullocky Point, about four kilometres from the city centre.

Older kids and parents should definitely visit the Defence of Darwin Experience ten minutes' drive away in East Point, where they can learn all about the Japanese invasion of the Top End and other Australian military history.

See out the day at Mindil Beach, where hundreds of people gather for amazing sunsets and a festive market on Thursdays and Sundays, from April to October. Although a tourist spotted a baby croc swimming off the shores of Mindil not too long ago, lifeguards ensure everybody is safe – despite what paranoid taxi drivers may say.

ULURU

Sunrise on a camel

 Age minimum: None, but given the cost, you may want to hold off on bringing the really tiny tots

 Open: Year round

 Visit: www.ayersrockresort.com.au

Uluru holds a special place in the hearts of many Australians. People talk about the energy of this sacred place, the quality of the light and the big rock's resonating significance.

I turned my second visit into a daddy-daughter getaway, and flew in directly from Melbourne with a five year old thirsty for any adventure, never mind visiting the most iconic landmark in the country.

Given the influx of tourists, the large resort that services Uluru operates like a well-oiled machine, from the hotel shuttle buses that greet passengers on arrival to accommodation and dining options for different budgets. While clinging to its outdated name, Ayers Rock Resort does an

excellent job of ensuring there are accommodation options for everyone, from the high-flying jetsetters to campervan families.

We treated ourselves to the

resort's Desert Gardens Hotel, where we enjoyed a room with a view of the mighty rock itself. Since it was too early for check-in, we hopped on the free shuttle bus to visit the Camel Farm, because no animal bats a long, droopy eyelash at a kid quite like a dromedary does.

After greeting the camels, water buffalo and emus, we booked a sunrise camel tour and headed to the resort Town Square. In person, Uluru looms larger than it does in the photos, although Raquel was less impressed with its spiritual and historical significance than she was with the opportunity to paint a boomerang and chat to a friendly artist in residence inside Wintjiri Arts + Museum. I parked her at a table and explored the exhibits and displays about the region's geology and cultural history.

Travelling with kids typically brings smiles and support from everyone you meet, and when you're a solo dad with a boisterous, curly-haired kid, you don't have to look hard for conversation or staff wanting to sweep her up and show her cool stuff.

After lunch at the Kulata Academy Cafe, we hopped on the bus in search of the shaded playground at the campground, the perfect place to burn off some energy safe from the sun rays baking the red outback earth.

A good play session later, Raquel fell asleep on the shuttle bus, exhausted from a very early morning start, the three-hour flight and the excitement of it all. I was happy to let her rest, because I had

signed us up for the 8.15pm Family Astro Tour that evening.

With the moon about ten per cent full, shimmering stars bloomed across the clear night sky. Stargazing is an extraordinary natural spectacle in this part of the world. An astronomer pointed out nebulas and the Galilean moons next to Jupiter, the different galaxies and constellations.

Towards the end, Raquel's sense of wonder was replaced by a fear of monsters lurking as shadows in the starlit trees. We grabbed takeaway noodles in the Town Square and retired early for the big day ahead.

When excited, young kids will wake up, put their clothes on, brush their teeth and do all the other stuff they usually *won't* do without a battle royale. Having already met the camels, the idea of riding one was made less exciting by the fact that it was dark and cold outside.

Wearing bright red ponchos, we rode atop a camel named Conner, ambling in single file along a well-worn path to a scenic lookout of Uluru. Definitely take your own camera and ask the friendly guides to snap a few pics, or be prepared to fork out for the third-party photographer who comes along for the ride.

After breakfast, it was off to the great rock itself, where we learned

more about the confusion that results when you're in Ayers Rock Resort with a surname that sounds remarkably similar to Ayers Rock.

That night, we visited the artist Bruce Munro's *Field of Light* exhibit, as thousands of LED lights lit up the outback, creating a mirror version of the stars above. The next day, we were back in Melbourne wondering if the whole thing had been a dream.

There are many different experiences available for families and visitors to Uluru and the under-rated Kata Tjuta. Depending on time and money, it would be foolish to try and do everything, although a three-day trip should give you plenty of time to say you've done it.

The heat ensures that most activities take place in the early morning or late afternoon, but there's cultural, culinary and art attractions to keep you busy in between. Having previously visited the region, I was happy to let Raquel dictate the pace for a change and follow her interests. It was encouraging to see that for my daughter, the true child of a travel writer, many of them overlapped with my own.

LITCHFIELD
NATIONAL PARK

Convenient wonders

 Age minimum: None

 Open: Dry season (May to October). Roads might be washed out and crocs might lurk in watering holes at other times

Visit: www.nt.gov.au/leisure/parks-reserves/find-a-park-to-visit/litchfield-national-park, also www.butterflyfarm.net.au

Of the two national parks that dominate most Top End itineraries, Litchfield is by far the most accessible.

Based in Darwin with the two young kids in tow, two hours of driving on the smooth 130-kilometres-an-hour road to Litchfield makes it an ideal spot for an overnight or weekend family getaway.

Litchfield's main attractions are close together, and are particularly great for the kids. The best time to visit is during the dry season (May to October), when the annoying bugs and annoyingly dangerous crocs clear out, and the roads become more accessible to rental cars.

For overnight accommodation, I found interesting reviews for a place called the Batchelor Butterfly Farm, located in the small town of Batchelor on the outskirts of the park. Owned and operated by an eccentric Irish/Filipino couple, the cabins feel more like a homestay. The property is home to various animals, including bunnies, pigs, goats and snakes; a fantastic restaurant; plenty of toys and books and that enthusiastic Territory hospitality.

The cabins are simple but spacious, the splash pool inviting, and the kids are encouraged to run amok. They loved the place and would gladly have stayed longer. From there, it's a short drive

orange mounds out of mud, saliva, faeces and plant material.

Built with ventilation to withstand the heat, predators and torrential rain, it's quite something to stand beneath an eight-metre-tall mound built by a creature that itself is less than one centimetre long.

With pipes and columns, these masterpieces are among the tallest non-human structures in the world. Visiting the mounds is a must, especially at sunset when they light up with that special orange-red tinge of the Top End.

The magnetic termite mounds, built by a different yet just as remarkable insect, resemble grey, uneven tombstone slabs inserted into the bush, perfectly aligned north to south.

into Litchfield, where we spotted the park's first natural attraction towering over the bush: cathedral termites have engineered gigantic

Further down the road are the park's closest aquatic wonders. Litchfield's waterfalls seem to offer something for everyone, from young hikers going rock jumping to older travellers content to soak up the natural beauty.

Croc-free, Wangi and Florence waterfalls are safe to swim in, providing an invigorating escape from the heat and a refreshing way to cool off after the hike to the base. There are no pram trails here, and if your kids are particularly clingy, you might want to move to a more accessible water attraction.

Closer to the highway, the Buley Rockholes is ideal for young kids still in floaties, as well as parents who are happy to spend a few hours lazing in the pristine pools. An artificial waterpark could not have designed a better aquatic playground, with launch pads for rock jumping, shallow pools for natural hydrotherapy and smooth rocks to lay out a picnic blanket.

Although there's no shortage of activities in the Top End, meeting butterflies and soaking in the unspoiled waters of Litchfield proved to be our most endearing highlight.

KAKADU
NATIONAL PARK

So much to see, so little time

 Age minimum: None

 Open: Dry season (May to October). Roads might be washed out and crocs might lurk in watering holes at other times

 Visit: www.parksaustralia.gov.au/kakadu

Rock art, waterfalls, gorges, swimming holes and wildlife in a protected area the size of European countries: it's easy to see why Kakadu draws the fascination it does.

A lot of people take in the park's highlights on a tour from Darwin, but given the length of the day, those tours don't generally accept toddlers and young kids. Which is perfectly fine, as it's easier to go at your own pace in your own vehicle, rented or otherwise.

To access the park from Darwin, it's about a three-hour drive, which can be broken up by activities and stops along the way (a morning cruise at the Corroboree Billabong is all but guaranteed to deliver wild croc action, as the system has the highest concentration of salties on the planet!).

Cruising on the long, fast and flat highway might well put the kids to sleep until you reach the park access at Jabiru. You'll definitely want to check out the Bowali Visitor Centre, which not only contains information and interactive boards about the park, but also has the latest updates about safe watering holes, guides, local activities and the bug situation.

Depending on what time you visit, the mozzies and midges can get hectic, and your tolerance for the elements will likely impact your decision to camp or stay in overnight accommodation. There are good options in Jabiru as well as the lovely Cooinda Lodge.

Kakadu has the world's highest concentration of Indigenous rock art. A half-hour's drive from Jabiru into the park is Nourlangie, home to the most famous and accessible rock art in the country. It's an

easy one-kilometre walk to the Anbangbang Gallery, where the art is on full display, and there are shaded areas too.

About an hour's drive north of Jabiru is Ubirr, the park's second major rock art gallery. Some of the pictograms here date back around 1500 years, and include images of the arrival of Europeans.

The track to the lookouts is rocky and steep, and might be too much for little ones, so a carrier would come in handy if you have one.

To access the most famous cascades – Gunlom, Jim Jim Falls and Twin Falls – prepare to do a lot of driving, some of it on unsealed roads. Gunlom is particularly toddler-friendly, with plenty of shallow spots in the swimming holes, and spacious sandy and grassy areas all serviced by a camp site with hot showers and flush toilets.

Given its size and wonders, we just scratched the surface of Kakadu. Suffice to say you'll need time to explore the park, and to allow the big sky, grand landscape and the natural and cultural wonders of the region to seduce you. By the time your kids have adjusted to the bush, you'll likely be heading back to Darwin.

Epilogue

If you think there's a lot to do at home – the laundry, the dishes, tidying up – imagine how much there is to do in Australia! This book is by no means definitive; most travellers know that the more you discover, the more things it

makes you want to discover. I could have written another book about the parks we visited, the beaches we lazed on and the scenic roads we cruised down. In fact, I did (please enjoy my shameless plug for *The Great Australian Bucket List*). This one focuses solely on the experiences of our children, but it would have been dishonest if I didn't get into the challenging nuts and bolts of family travel. I hope you find the various tips and tricks useful, or at the very least, not too discouraging. I wanted to be honest.

If you follow family travel blogs and social media channels, you seldom hear about the sleepless nights and nightmare flights, the meltdowns, food disasters and nappy catastrophes. Everything always looks so peachy! But you can bet those carefully manicured parents and their immaculately smiling kids are *also* travelling through the outer suburbs of Hell, and a lot more frequently than what you might see on their Instagram accounts. Children, bless them, are the great democratiser. They don't care how rich you are, how fancy the restaurant is, how lucky they are to be there or how good it will look if they just smile in the photo. Their needs are immediate and powerful, and their honest insights can slice to the bone. You've got to love them for all of it, not least because the world becomes fresh and startlingly interesting when you see it through their eyes. For all the challenges they might bring to the travelling family table, when kids are learning, laughing and delighting in the experiences around them, it sends shockwaves of joy into a parent's heart. Of course, you already know this.

The jury is out whether our own year of travelling across Australia (and later Southeast Asia) will result in our kids being smarter, more engaged, more social and more accepting of cultures around them. We know the experience will definitely leave a mark, and as with all parents, we just have to wait with hope to see what that mark is. If nothing else, I urge you to consider this very simple teaching about achieving happiness: find something meaningful to do, someone to love and something exciting to look forward to. If a big family adventure doesn't tick all those boxes, nothing will.

Acknowledgements

There's an African proverb that says it takes a village to raise a child, and it takes a lot of great people, companies and organisations to put a book like this together.

Sponsors

A very special thank you to the amazing sponsors who made this book possible: Ford Australia, Oaks Hotels and Resorts, Discovery Holiday Parks, Jetstar Airways, World Expeditions, Sunshades Eyewear, Move Yourself!, Journey Beyond, Britax, Keen Footwear, Valcobaby, Swiss Gear Luggage, Tourism and Events Queensland and Tourism Tasmania.

Our enduring gratitude to Jasmine Moberak, Eddy Sleiman, Ingrid Nason, Simon Tsang, Kellie Ogilvie, Stacey Beckingham, Kira Klein, Larissa Duncomb, Brad Atwal, Danielle Flegg, Sue Badyari, Jane Ford, Rob Cowie, Anthony Whittle, Jami Sutcliffe, Caitlin Jones, Jessica Schmidt, Jeffrey New, Teresa Thompson and Debra Gaul.

Affirm Press

It was my publisher's idea to bring the family along on my adventure to Australia, where I researched and recorded what that experience was like as I ticked off *The Great Australian Bucket List*. I don't think I quite realised what I was getting myself into, but that describes parenting in general. Special thanks to Keiran Rogers, Martin Hughes, Ruby Ashby-Orr, Grace Breen, Laura McNicol Smith, Stephanie Bishop-Hall, Emily Ashendon, Freya Horton Andrews, Jaclyn Crupi and all at Affirm Press, as well as Maria Biaggini and Ann Wilson from Post Pre-press Group.

Our support

Thank you to our friends and family, Down Under and in the Great White North. The Kalmeks, the Vovos, Bobba and Zeida, the Radus family, the Resnik family, Ron and Ron and Renicia Gordon, Faye, Jon and Rachel Rothbart, the Barons, the Villagomezs, the Aikens, Annette and Issy Liebenthal, Erin and Michaela.

Thanks as always to Dave Rock for the videos, and to Karen Anderson for the website help. Thank you to the travelling Van Viegens! We really could not have done any of this without Raquel and Gali's soul aunties, Jaci Taylor and Amy Markus – and they know it! And to Katherine Droga, who provided just the shot-in-the-arm the project (and our weary souls) needed.

And of course, thank you to my wife, Ana, who agreed to embark on this crazy adventure in the first place.

In Victoria

Glenn Harvey, Sharon Wells, Kellie Barrett, Roland Pick, Samantha Mackley, Brook Powell, Shane Brown, Tim Whittaker, Sheena Dang, the National Trust of Australia, staff at the Oaks Southbank, the Melbourne Museum, John Rundell, Judith Henke at the Melbourne Zoo and Visit Victoria.

In Western Australia

Emily Andrews, Shark Bay Hotel, Wendy Mann, Fran Raven, Stell Limnios and Chloe Lyons at the lovely Attika Hotel, Lily Yeang and Australia's South West, Beth and Rick Cowan at the lovely Bridgewater B&B in Margaret River, Karl and Sharon Rost, Prince Graeme in Hutt River, Sean Stahlhut at Fremantle Prison YHA, Ron and Renicia Gordon.

In Tasmania

Mark and Claire Walsh at Discovery Parks Cradle Mountain, Narissa Armstrong at Devonport Discovery Parks, Genevieve Hall.

In South Australia

Robert Main, The Barn, Suzanne Parisi and the South Australian Tourism Commission, Dylan Beach at Monarto Zoo, Yasmin and Georgia Stehr, Cheryl Turner, Jane Ford, the staff at the Oaks Embassy.

In New South Wales

Kristine McCarthy, Danielle Edwards, Kelly Seagrave, Kellie Sommerville at Crystal Castle, Louise Wallace at Scenic World, Kirk Tutt, Michelle Baker, Toni at Toboggan Hill, Lia Pereira, the staff at the Oaks Goldsbrough, Oaks Pacific Blue and Oaks Cypress Lakes.

In the Australian Capital Territory

Donna Ciaccia and Joanne Barges at Visit Canberra, Glen Nagle, Heather Gow-Carey at Tidbinbilla Nature Reserve.

In Queensland

Georgie Sadler, the unstoppable Peter Hackworth, Peta Zcitsch, Dave and Georgina at Discovery Parks Fraser Coast, Biccara Guerin, Janelle Murray, Caitlin Jones, Brett and Hilton Abkin, Amanda Perry and the CaPTA Group, Discovery Parks Airlie Beach, Oaks Sunshine Coast, Oaks Charlotte Towers Brisbane, the Oaks Lagoons Port Douglas and the Oaks Rivermarque Mackay.

In the Northern Territory

Leanna Boyd, the Caravan Industry Association of Australia, Merryn Andrews, Karena Noble, Caitlin Jones, Oaks Elan Darwin.

Photo Credits

COVER
Clockwise from top left:
Heleen Van Assche /
Shutterstock.com
Robin Esrock
Robin Esrock
Ana Esrock
Robin Esrock
Tap10 / Shutterstock.com
Ana Esrock
Robin Esrock
Tropical studio / Shutterstock.com

INTERNALS
iv: Robin Esrock

INTRODUCTION
4: Esrock World Media
7: Robin Esrock
8: Robin Esrock
9 (left): Robin Esrock
9 (right): Esrock World Media
10: Esrock World Media

Fear of Flying with Kids
12: Freepik.com
13: Robin Esrock
14: Ana Esrock
15: Robin Esrock
16: Robin Esrock
18: Robin Esrock
19: Robin Esrock

VICTORIA
Eureka Skydeck
21: Robin Esrock
22: Esrock World Media
23: Robin Esrock
24: Ana Esrock

Melbourne Zoo Roar'n'Snore
25: Esrock World Media
26: Robin Esrock
27: Robin Esrock
28: Esrock World Media

Melbourne Museum and Scienceworks
29: Robin Esrock
30: Robin Esrock
31: Robin Esrock

National Gallery of Victoria (NGV)
32: Robin Esrock
33: Robin Esrock
34: Robin Esrock

Game Day at the MCG
35: Robin Esrock
36: Robin Esrock
37: Robin Esrock
38: Robin Esrock
Sovereign Hill
39: Esrock World Media
40: Robin Esrock
41: Ana Esrock
42: Robin Esrock

ArtPlay
43: ArtPlay, City of Melbourne
44: ArtPlay, City of Melbourne
45: ArtPlay, City of Melbourne
Bright Bathing Boxes
46: Robin Esrock
47: Robin Esrock

Ashcombe Maze & Lavender Gardens
48: Courtesy Ashcombe Maze and Lavender Gardens
49: Robin Esrock
50 (bottom): Robin Esrock
50 (top) PENDING Courtesy A Maze'N Things

Peninsula Hot Springs
51: Robin Esrock
52: Robin Esrock
53: Robin Esrock
54 (top and bottom): Robin Esrock

Phillip Island
55: Robin Esrock

56 (top): Ana Esrock
56 (bottom): Robin Esrock
57: Robin Esrock
58 (top): Robin Esrock
58 (bottom): Anna Esrock
59 (top): Courtesy Phillip Island Nature Parks
59 (bottom): Robin Esrock

Puffing Billy
60: Robin Esrock
61: Robin Esrock
62: Courtesy Puffing Billy

Central Deborah Gold Mine
63: Courtesy Bendigo Heritage Attractions
64: Esrock World Media
65: Esrock World Media

Fairy Park
66: Ana Esrock
67: Ana Esrock
68 (both): Ana Esrock
69 (both): Ana Esrock

The Great Ocean Road
70: Pixabay.com
71: Robin Esrock
72: Robin Esrock
73: Robin Esrock

Where to Stay
74 (top): Freepik.com
75: Robin Esrock
76 (top): Robin Esrock
76 (bottom): Robin Esrock
77: Robin Esrock
80: Robin Esrock
81: Robin Esrock
82: Illustrations by Cristina Gambaccini
83: Robin Esrock

SOUTH AUSTRALIA
87: Robin Esrock

Oceanic Visitor
88: Courtesy Oceanic Victor

374

89: Ana Esrock
90 (top): Robin Esrock
90 (bottom): Esrock World Media
91: Robin Esrock

Kangaroo Island
92: Robin Esrock
93: Robin Esrock
94: Robin Esrock
95: Robin Esrock

Haigh's Chocolates
96: Robin Esrock
97: Ana Esrock
98: Robin Esrock

Silver Sands Beach
99: Robin Esrock
100 (top and bottom): Robin Esrock
101: Robin Esrock

Monarto Zoo's Lions 360
102: Robin Esrock
103: Robin Esrock
104: Robin Esrock
105: Robin Esrock

Adelaide Central Market
106: Robin Esrock
107: Robin Esrock
108: Robin Esrock

Cleland Wildlife Park
109: Robin Esrock
110: Robin Esrock
111: Robin Esrock

The Garden of Unearthly Delights
112: Robin Esrock
113: Robin Esrock
114: Ana Esrock

Glenelg
115: Esrock World Media
116: Robin Esrock
117: Ana Esrock

Blue Lake and Ewens Ponds
118: Robin Esrock
119: Robin Esrock
120: Robin Esrock

The Naracoorte Caves
121: Ana Esrock

122: Robin Esrock
123: Robin Esrock
124-125: Illustration by Cristina Gambaccini

Pack Like a Pro
126: Freepik.com
127: Robin Esrock
128: Robin Esrock
129: Robin Esrock
131: Ana Esrock
132: Robin Esrock
133: Ana Esrock
134: Robin Esrock

WESTERN AUSTRALIA
137: Robin Esrock

Margaret River
138: Robin Esrock
139: Esrock World Media
140 (top and bottom): Robin Esrock
141: Robin Esrock

Principality of Hutt River
142: Robin Esrock
143: Robin Esrock
144 (top and bottom): Robin Esrock
145: Robin Esrock

WA Maritime Museum
146: Ana Esrock
147: Esrock World Media
148 (top and bottom): Robin Esrock
149: Ana Esrock

Caversham Wildlife Park
150: Robin Esrock
151: Ana Esrock
152 (top and bottom): Robin Esrock
153: Robin Esrock

Rottnest Island
154: Ana Esrock
155: Robin Esrock
156 (top): Esrock World Media
156 (bottom): Robin Esrock
157: Robin Esrock

Kings Park:
158: Pixabay.com

159: Esrock World Media
160: Esrock World Media

Ocean Park Aquarium, Shell Beach and Hamelin Pool
161: Robin Esrock
162: Ana Esrock
163: Robin Esrock
164 (left and right): Robin Esrock

Monkey Mia
165: Robin Esrock
166 (top and bottom): Robin Esrock
167: Robin Esrock
168: Joanna Nelson-Hauer / Shutterstock.com

Valley of the Giants
169: Ana Esrock
170 (top and bottom): Robin Esrock
171: Ana Esrock
172: Robin Esrock

The Jewel Cave
173: Robin Esrock
174: Robin Esrock
175: Robin Esrock

The Old Marron Farm
176: Robin Esrock
177 (top and bottom): Robin Esrock
178 (top): Robin Esrock
178 (bottom): Esrock World Media
179 (top and bottom): Robin Esrock

National Anzac Centre
180: Robin Esrock
181: Robin Esrock
182: Robin Esrock

The Gap and Natural Bridge
183: Robin Esrock
184 (top and bottom): Robin Esrock
185: Robin Esrock

On the Road
186: Freepik.com
187: Robin Esrock
188: Robin Esrock

191: Robin Esrock
192: Robin Esrock
195: Hadrian / Shutterstock.
com
196: Robin Esrock
197: Robin Esrock

TASMANIA
199: Courtesy Bridestowe
Lavender Fields

The Museum of Old and New Art
200: Robin Esrock
201: Robin Esrock
202: Courtesy MONA
203 (top): Courtesy MONA
203 (bottom): Robin Esrock

Cradle Mountain
204: Jaci Taylor
205: Robin Esrock
206: Jaci Taylor
207 (top and bottom): Robin
Esrock

Devils @ Cradle
208: Robin Esrock
209: Robin Esrock
210: Robin Esrock
211: Robin Esrock

Bridestowe Lavender Estate
212: Courtesy Bridestowe
Lavender Fields
213 (top and bottom): Ana
Esrock
214: Ana Esrock
215 (top): Courtesy Bridestowe
Lavender Fields
215 (bottom): Ana Esrock

Tasmazia & the Village of Lower Crackpot
216: Ana Esrock
217: Ana Esrock
218 (top and bottom): Ana
Esrock
219 (top and bottom): Ana
Esrock

Eating Out and Dining In
220: Freepik.com

221 (top and bottom): Robin
Esrock
222: Robin Esrock
223: Robin Esrock
224: Ana Esrock
225 (all): Robin Esrock
226 (all): Robin Esrock
227 (all): Robin Esrock
228 (all): Robin Esrock
229 (left and right): Robin
Esrock
229 (centre): Ana Esrock
230 (all): Robin Esrock
231: Robin Esrock

NEW SOUTH WALES
233: Robin Esrock

Sydney Fish Market
234: Robin Esrock
235: Robin Esrock
236 (top): Esrock World Media
236 (bottom): Robin Esrock
237: Robin Esrock

Bondi Beach
238: Robin Esrock
239: Robin Esrock
240: Robin Esrock

Darling Harbour
241: Pixabay.com
242: Ana Esrock
243 (top and bottom): Ana
Esrock

Blue Mountains
244: Esrock World Media
245: Robin Esrock
246: Robin Esrock
247 (top): Esrock World Media
247 (bottom): Robin Esrock

Treetops Adventures
248: Robin Esrock
249: Robin Esrock
250 (top and bottom): Robin
Esrock

Irukandji Shark & Ray Encounters
251: Robin Esrock
252 (top and bottom): Robin
Esrock

253: Robin Esrock
254: Robin Esrock
Toboggan Hill Park
255: Robin Esrock
256 (top and bottom): Robin
Esrock
257: Robin Esrock

Hunter Valley Gardens
258: Robin Esrock
259: Robin Esrock
260 (top and bottom): Robin
Esrock
261 (top and bottom): Robin
Esrock

Byron Bay
262: Robin Esrock
263: Robin Esrock
264: Ana Esrock
265: Robin Esrock

Crystal Castle
266: Robin Esrock
267: Ana Esrock
268 (top): Robin Esrock
268 (bottom): Ana Esrock
269: Esrock World Media

Money Matters
270: Freepik.com
271: Robin Esrock
272: crbellette / Shutterstock.
com
273: Nature1000 /
Shutterstock
274: POC / Shutterstock.com

AUSTRALIAN CAPITAL TERRITORY
277: Ana Esrock

Questacon
278: Robin Esrock
279: Ana Esrock
280: Robin Esrock
281 (top and bottom): Robin
Esrock

Canberra Deep Space Communication Complex
282: Robin Esrock
283: Robin Esrock
284: Robin Esrock

285: Ana Esrock

Tidbinbilla Nature Reserve
286: Robin Esrock
287: Robin Esrock
288: Robin Esrock

National Dinosaur Museum
289: Ana Esrock
290: Ana Esrock
291 (top and bottom): Ana Esrock

Cockington Green Gardens
292: Robin Esrock
293: Robin Esrock
294 (top and bottom): Robin Esrock
295: Robin Esrock

Be Smart with Screens
296: Freepiks.com
297: Robin Esrock
298: Ana Esrock
299: Robin Esrock
300: Robin Esrock
301: Esrock World Media
302: Robin Esrock

QUEENSLAND
305: Robin Esrock

Eat Street Northshore
306: Robin Esrock
307: Robin Esrock
308 (top and bottom): Robin Esrock
309 (top and bottom); Robin Esrock

Jungle Surfing
310: Robin Esrock
311: Robin Esrock
312: Robin Esrock
313: Robin Esrock

Wildlife Habitat
314: Robin Esrock
315: Robin Esrock
316 (top and bottom): Robin Esrock
317: Robin Esrock

Mackay
318: Robin Esrock
320: Ana Esrock

Cap Hillsborough
321: Robin Esrock
322: Robin Esrock
323: Robin Esrock

Whitehaven Beach
324: Robin Esrock
325: Robin Esrock
326: Robin Esrock
327: Robin Esrock

Fraser Island
328: Robin Esrock
329: Esrock World Media
330: Robin Esrock
331 (top): Robin Esrock
331 (bottom): Ana Esrock

South Bank Parklands
332: Martin Valigursky / Shutterstock.com
333: Robin Esrock
334 (top and bottom): Robin Esrock

Rainforestation Nature Park
335: Robin Esrock
336: Robin Esrock
337: Robin Esrock
338 (top and bottom): Robin Esrock

Hudsons Circus
339: Robin Esrock
340: Ana Esrock
341: Robin Esrock

Staying Healthy
342: my_ photos / Shutterstock.com
344: Robin Esrock
345: Robin Esrock

NORTHERN TERRITORY
347: Robin Esrock
348: Courtesy Crocosaurus Cove
349: Robin Esrock
350: Robin Esrock
351 (top): Robin Esrock
351 (bottom): Robin Esrock

Museum and Art Gallery of the Northern Territory
352: Robin Esrock

353: Robin Esrock
354: Robin Esrock

Uluru
355: Robin Esrock
356 (top and bottom): Robin Esrock
357: Robin Esrock
358: Esrock World Media
359: Robin Esrock

Litchfield National Park
360: Ana Esrock
361: Robin Esrock
362 (top and bottom): Robin Esrock
363: Robin Esrock

Kakadu National Park
364: Neale Cousland/ Shutterstock.com
365: Trial / Shutterstock.com
366: Julien DESTRES / Shutterstock
367: Pixabay.com
368: Robin Esrock
361: Courtesy Crocosaurus Cove
374: Robin Esrock

Also by Robin Esrock

For over a decade, renowned travel journalist, bestselling author and TV host Robin Esrock scoured the globe in search of one-of-a-kind, bucket list–worthy experiences. During his remarkable journey to over 100 countries on seven continents, Esrock uncovered unique adventures, fascinating histories, cultural spectacles, natural wonders, hilarious situations and unforgettable characters – proving that modern travel is so much more than just over-trafficked tourist attractions. With his trademark wit, photography and insight, Esrock introduces the inspiring experiences you'll be talking and dreaming about for many years to come.

About the Author

Robin Esrock is a bestselling author, journalist, television host, public speaker and producer. His stories and photography have appeared in major publications on five continents including *National Geographic Traveler*, *The Guardian*, *The Chicago Tribune*, *South China Morning Post* and *The Globe and Mail*. Robin has been profiled as a travel expert by *60 Minutes*, ABC, *The Sydney Morning Herald*, MSNBC and *The Wall St Journal*, and he was honoured as Master of Ceremonies at the Explorer's Club Annual Dinner in New York. The creator and co-host of the 40-part television series *Word Travels*, Robin has seen his adventures broadcast in over 100 countries on National Geographic and Travel Channel International. He is the bestselling author of *The Great Australian Bucket List* and *The Great Global Bucket List*. Robin lives in Vancouver, Canada, with his wife and two children.

Visit him online at www.robinesrock.com.